T0099773

THE GODDESS RETURNS TO EARTH

Feminine & Masculine Aspects Must Balance

Presenters: Jesus/Yeshua, Divine Mother, Father-Mother God, Saint Germain, Lady Nada, Kuthumi-Agrippa, AA Michael,

Verling CHAKO Priest, Ph.D.

Cover layout by Author & daughter, Susan Verling Miller O'Brien & grandson, Adam Miller Schwartz. The portrait is Chako at 5 years old.

Order this book online at www.trafford.com
or email orders@trafford.com

Most Trafford titles are also available at major online book retailers.

Printed in the United States of America.

ISBN: 978-1-4269-3563-3 (soft)
ISBN: 978-1-4269-3564-0 (ebook)

Trafford rev. 6/22/2010

www.trafford.com

North America & international
toll-free: 1 888 232 4444 (USA & Canada)
phone: 250 383 6864 • fax: 812 355 4082

PREVIOUS BOOKS

The Ultimate Experience, the Many Paths to God series:

REALITIES of the CRUCIFIXION (2006)

MESSAGES from the HEAVENLY HOSTS (2007)

YOUR SPACE BROTHERS and SISTERS GREET YOU! (2008)

TEACHINGS of the MASTERS of LIGHT (2008)

PAULUS of TARSUS (2010)

To the Goddesses in my life, Susan, Sandra, and Sara, my heart glows as I watch you bring balance within your Being.

ACKNOWLEDGEMENTS

My first acknowledgment is always to Yeshua. I consider our books **his** books for it is he who brings in the topic and then brings forth the many Masters who give us their wisdom on the subject. Therefore, thank you, one and all. It has been my honor to be your scribe.

Heather Clarke is my next recipient of heartfelt thanks for she is my editor. She catches my typos, too many or lack of commas, and suggests other ways to say the same thing as my telepathy falters at times, and I have convoluted a sentence or phrase (especially when turning a tape over). She is the founder of the Arizona Enlightenment Center and consequently very busy. I appreciate the time she devotes to me and my books, many times working on a chapter in the wee hours of the morning. Thank you, dear friend, for all you do.

Susan Verling Miller O'Brien is my computer helpmate. She is the one who frames my books. She places my files of the chapters into the Table of Contents and sees that all is in order. In other words, when she is finished with the task, I have a book! I thank you, dear heart; it is obvious how much your expertise is needed (*chuckles*).

I have a new member of my team to thank. He is my grandson, Adam Miller Schwartz. He is a very talented Graphic Artist in Boston. It is his creative work you see for the covers of this book. I thank you for taking the time to design such beautiful covers. I am blessed to have you as a member of my family.

Dear Readers, I give all of you my deepest thanks also. Your dedication in buying and reading our books is so gratifying. You are much needed in this equation of expanding outward the wisdom of the Masters. Blessings to all, Chako.

PREFACE

In February 2010 I had an early morning dream that went like this: *I was standing, facing the end of my bed. There was a man sitting at the foot of my bed. He had a slim black mustache, showing me that he was a man. He said to me "draw to you the Queen of Hearts." Then he said "ask Jesus to help you..."* I lost the rest of the sentence as I awoke. But as I was awakening, he made a third statement: *"the end is near."*

Yeshua held his monthly class via Cynthia Williams at my house on February 21st. I told him about the dream and asked for his interpretation. I knew the *Queen of Hearts* is the Divine Mother, but I wanted to know the meaning of drawing her to me and just what was Jesus/Yeshua teaching me? I also knew that the *end is near* was about the ascension.

Yeshua told me that the Queen of Hearts is the Goddess energy returning to the planet and that we would be writing a book about this soon. On Wednesday, March 10th my ninth book was launched and indeed the title is *The Goddess Returns to Earth.* This entire book has only that one theme, the importance of balancing the feminine and masculine aspects within us.

As he taught on this subject that day, we students were hard pressed to make sense of some of the statements: *if you are a male, you will return as a female and if you are a woman in this lifetime, you will return as a man.* I can imagine, Readers, that you too may be bewildered. In order to help in your understanding a bit more, I have put the full teaching that he gave on that subject in the Appendix, with the kind permission of Cynthia Williams, voice-channel *extraordinaire.*

This book will stretch you, Readers. Blessings, Chako.

Contents

INTRODUCTION

I AM Yeshua, known as Jesus the Christ: *I come to you this morning for we are going to start our ninth book. It will be a book on creating for Humanity the purpose and the idea that we are One. How do we come to that position? How do we get to where you, yourself, will say we are One?*

In order to be One with the Father and your own consciousness, people need to be One with themselves, within their own body. They need to know that they carry the two principals, the feminine and masculine (aspects). They need to know that these must come into balance so that one is not dominant over the other. This can only be done with intent and purpose and consciousness and Light. (Only then) can one become conscious. It is by bringing in new ideas, by listening to your wisdom, by bringing in more Light to light up the shadow parts of you. Each body has its shadow; each body has its Light in order to shine into those dark spaces within.

Some people do not wish to have their shadow brought forth. They do not want to bother with the work that is entailed. They would prefer to just go on their merry way or maybe not so merry way and let the chips fall where they may.

As you know, Readers, it takes all kinds. Each person has his or her own consciousness, his or her own way of doing things and looking at the world. However, it is the ***intent*** *of the heart that will make the difference. Just as this Channel expressed the intent to start a new book, one must have the intent to bring about more consciousness, the intent to learn more about oneself, to learn more about what makes a person tick, we'll say.*

Why do you act like you do? Is it because you are acting like your parents programmed you to be? Is that really you, or is that a mimic of your father or a mimic of your mother? Are you truly doing what you wished to do—what your contract said—or are you still just being in someone else's shadow?

Humanity has walked the Earth for millions of years. It was not always in a form that you would recognize. You came from the sea. You were Sea-People first and human second. People think of themselves as only human and do not realize that they had other forms. It may shock you to know that I was a Merman and others were Mermaids, but we carried great intelligence. Intelligence and your sense of wisdom come from the sea creatures of the deep, your whales and dolphins. They knew how to bring that Oneness to them. They knew they were important to a group, to a pod, but they also knew they were important to themselves.

I have given you a little taste this morning of what this book will be about. It is bringing your principal, your Goddess to the forefront. You men have a difficult time in acknowledging the feminine parts of yourselves. That is why Beings ask for homosexual lives so that they could learn the differences. Lesbians want to know the masculine principal and the gays wish to know the feminine principal. No one is wrong. Each has a purpose—a learning purpose.

This morning I will be bringing forth another Being. He is wise beyond measure and he will be starting the book, for this is the Introduction. And as I have said, the book will be on the principals of bringing back the Goddess to humanity. Up to this time it has been a Patriarch society. The Patriarch smothered the Mother part—the Matriarch. It made her subservient.

Consequently, there were more wars because it was the masculine principal that was in charge. However, the Goddess is coming forth, the Goddess of love, of beautiful arts and creations, the feminine aspect of people. Therefore, that will balance out the more aggressive males.

Let me step back now and let this great Being speak.

Good morning my children, **I AM Sanat Kumara.** I am quite ancient and I will be teaching you this morning about the feminine principal. You have heard many times, I am sure, that you must bring a balance into your body. People do not know how to do that. If you are a man, you do manly things. If you are a woman, you do womanly things. It is only when a man ventures into the woman's domain that he gets a taste of that energy when decorating the interior of a house, or being a fabulous cook—cooking, baking and decorating beautiful cake creations.

When you see these people on your television, they are into their feminine principal. There is one television show, however, where the star of the cooking show is an angry teacher, an angry cook. He does that for show, for ratings. However, what it does is light up the fact that he is coming from his masculine, dominant side as he intimidates all the other cooks on the TV show with his anger and disgust over the other cooks' creations.

However, there are many cooks on television who are women. They use the masculine parts of themselves in order to be the star of the show, following the time-period allowed to them in order to present their creations—(*in an orderly fashion, presenting mouth-watering meals, versus a chaotic form).* Therefore, she has blended her masculine and feminine energies.

A long time ago, and I mean thousands of years ago, a different principal of masculine or feminine energy populated the Earth. Before the population of the Earth, there were the Sea People. There was blend there. But as they came forth and took human bodies, they then lost that Oneness. It lessened. They found that they had to be one or the other—either masculine energy in a male's body or feminine energy in a female's body. They did not know how to blend. So you see, evolution is a long process.

Now people are apt to want a Biblical discussion here. They are going to want me to say *God created this and God created that* and that is true. However, keep in mind that He also created the seas and He created the Sea People. There is a wonderful woman Channel, Cynthia Williams. She is from the sea. She teaches and brings in many of the Sea People, making the dolphin sounds. There will come a time when people will return to the sea. Water will once again cover the world. It will be a gradual evolution, but it will happen. You have that phrase, *ashes to ashes* or *dust to dust.* Well this is *water to water.* First there was water, then there was land and now there will be water again—*water to water.* Sea People will reign once again. That, you see, is for Planet Earth. Planet Earth was always a water-world.

There was a movie out with Kevin Costner telling of the water-world after destruction had come to the planet. Once again what is shown are all the wars, always fighting. Would it not be more enjoyable, more desirable to live in peace and harmony again? This can only happen when the basic principals of the masculine and feminine are joined. One is not dominant over the other. Your world now is struggling, for change must happen. It is the birthing of the Goddess, the feminine principal, like a chick that is pecking its way out of its shell.

Whenever there is a massive change that is upon you, there will be struggles and fights as people recalibrate their existence. Those who cannot keep up make their transition—they die and they will either come back to this world or they will go to other places.

The process is upon you; you cannot avoid it. My friend Blue Star of the Pleiades has told people so many times to get off that fence (*and make a choice one way or another*). It is almost too late now. For you see if you just sit on the fence you really have made a choice. Your choice is to make **no** choice. That is very dangerous; it is dangerous to your growth. It is dangerous to your spiritual life, for when you make no choice you are saying *I will go whichever way the wind blows.* If it blows me off the fence this way or blows me off the fence that way—whichever way the wind blows, I will go. Now there are people who do that but it is not a particularly productive way of living. They need a purpose; they need intent for *doing* and *being.* Let that purpose be one of advancement, to evolve, to step upon another rung of the ladder, to bring more wisdom and knowledge to one. There needs to be love; there needs to be a passion for life.

All of you Readers have asked for consciousness, for growth, or you would not be reading these books. You have asked for this; you have asked.

I AM Sanat Kumara and I come to you this morning to give you this brief pep talk. You are Light; you are love. Keep the fulfillment of your contracts. Be ready to go forth with purpose—the purpose in love, always love.

I bless you. I AM Sanat Kumara.

(*Thank you, Lord.*)

You are welcome, dear child, you are welcome.

Jeshua: *All right, dear one, do you wish to continue? (Yes, please.) We have come today with the purpose of setting the tone for this ninth book. It will most likely be the last book, although never say "never." As the energies of the world speed up, it may not be possible to have another book published. We will see.*

Now we will move forward and give you our wisdom. I will say that birthing a book is a privilege for us also for it gives us an avenue, an arena to tell our thoughts and wisdom to people. If we had no vehicle in which to come forth and speak our words and if we had no one to scribe these words, then there would be a gap in Humanity's growth. We have one Channel writing a book. Now multiply that by thousands and you can see how the energy and wisdom will spread out. It must go forth. This Channel may not realize it, but she could also collaborate with another Channel and they could bring forth a book together. We shall see. (Author: consequently, I ran this idea by Cynthia Williams and she received instant validation that we ***will be*** *co-authoring a book (Book 10, out this Fall) in the not too distant future. (Yeshua wishes to tell his story)*

I am drawing this to a close for now. I will speak more at another date. (When do you wish me to sit again?) Whenever you wish to...

I AM Yeshua

(Thank you, Lord).

You are welcome.

Good morning, my precious one, I AM Yeshua. We will continue our book that we started on Wednesday (3-10-10). I suggest, my dearest one, to just let the energy flow. Do not worry so as to whether it is Me, or your higher self, or your personality. Just let the energy flow. You and I are One as you have been told. Therefore, your thoughts are my thoughts. We are joined. You are an Aspect of me. We are One.

I wish to continue this introductory chapter, for it is not completed. Last time at the beginning we had the Lord Sanat Kumara speak. We were speaking about the importance of defining your position on that fence. Have you gotten off of it? Have you made a choice? Are you being Light and love or are you still dallying with the shadow? Have you made a decision as to your feminine and masculine principals no matter what sex you are? You must carry these two principals. They must be joined. They must be balanced.

This book is not meant to be what is termed "pabulum" as if it is not worth reading—it's not worth mentioning. It is spoken and written in a very simplistic manner, for Humanity makes things way too complicated. With simplicity, people are apt to think they are being fed pabulum—the mush that is given to babies. Whereas if they would look deeper, they would see that what we are giving them is esoteric knowledge that has been in the Ethers for eons of time.

I have told you that we are all from the sea. We are Sea People. If you wish to read more about this, you need to go to Cynthia Williams' website (www.dolphinheartjourneys.com) where she speaks of the dolphins and takes people out to sea to swim with the dolphins. She channels the Pod of One. She is a magnificent sea creature in a human body. I will go a step further and say ***you all are sea creatures in a human body.*** *(One may even have had* *a past life as an octopus!) Now if that does not change some theological mind sets, I do not know how else to shock people. It is a mind set, a belief system that you have been taught since you have been human. You were taught by your parents, teachers, and church leaders. You have been told repeatedly about your religion. Therefore, you are quite programmed in the ways of the physical world. Consequently, you are still babes in arms when it comes to remembering your roots—remembering that you are from the sea.*

This Channel and Cynthia will be collaborating on a book, and we will talk about the origins of the Sea People, for that was your beginnings on this planet.

Those of you who are millions of years old have come from other planets. You took up habitation there. You would be different from people on this Earth.

You have been all things; you have been all colors. You have been rocks; you have been reptiles; you have been animals. (You have been trees and frogs.) And you have been humans. You have been all things.

At the end cycle of those lives, you had to remember where your roots were. That is where you are in this life time. You are remembering. You will have past life dreams that will help you to remember. The dreams most likely will not make much sense to you for they will be full of metaphors and symbols. However, they are to awaken you as you remember.

The Goddess, dear friends, is upon the planet right now—the energy of the Goddess, the nurturing, the intuition, and the caring are becoming stronger on the planet.

It must, you see, otherwise the planet would become a warring planet such as Mars was. It can only end in destruction.

Man loves war. They love the power, especially if they are the leaders of it. They love the resources that they pillage, especially if they are the leaders of that war.

Therefore, in the great Father's wisdom, He sends forth the Goddess energy again—the Goddess that will merge with the masculine principal and bring all back into the balance of peace.

Why would you think there could be peace when the masculine and feminine principals are so far apart? The masculine is the war; the feminine Goddess is the peace. They must come together; they must be balanced.

There is great ado about the prophecy of 1000 years of peace. What it is actually addressing is the 1000 years of the Goddess energy. There still will be skirmishes, for the masculine is always rearing its head, trying to be dominant again. But on the whole, the planet will have peace because it will be a planet of balance and a planet of Goddess energy. People will be more intuitive. They will carry more awareness. They will have a greater consciousness.

You see, the masculine can only go so far before it becomes so literal, so left-brained, and so intellectual that Humanity then starts to lose its right-brain significance. It starts to lose its spiritual awareness. That is what is lacking today—the spiritual awareness versus the religious dogma. Your religions carry such dogma. Each sect thinking it is the only correct way; ***it*** *is the only correct way. None of them, as shocking as it sounds, none of them is the right way, including Christianity, including Judaism, including Islamic ideologies.* ***None*** *of them is the right way for the right way is total spirituality with the Father—with All That Is. It is not Jesus; it is the Father. It is not Mohammed; it is the Father. It is not Abraham; it is the Father. The Father is the right way. And of course it is the Mother—the Mother, the Holy Spirit; the Mother, the Holy Essence, that part of God.*

Do you not think if there is a Consciousness so advanced that It made masculine and feminine bodies, do you not think It too would carry the two essences? Of course It would. It would be Father; It would be Mother.

I wish now to bring in one of the Divine energies. You will know her as Mary Magdalene. I know her as my lover, my wife, as my Ray, as my twin flame, as the other part of me. Therefore, I will step back now and let her come forth.

Good morning my precious Readers, **I AM Mary Magdalene** here once again. I am smiling, for it gives me such pleasure to come and give you Readers my viewpoints on different subjects. The subject for this book of course will be varied, but the main theme is about the Goddess energy.

As many of you know while some may not know, I carried that energy. I was that (Goddess) energy on this planet. Yeshua speaks of himself as a Merman who came to change the DNA of the hu-man. I was at his side even then. I was the Mermaid who came to help the Merman to change the DNA in the hu-man.

As you see, when we became human then, we took on the human trials and tribulations, we'll say. You have been told in different readings, although it may have been Yeshua speaking through Cynthia Williams that 75% of your karma is Humanity's karma. I believe we wrote about this in one of our books. Therefore, the other 25% is your personal karma. It then requires you to not only transmute your karma but to help to transmute all of the karma you created as human beings. Therefore, when

Yeshua and I were in the human bodies, we too had to work with and transmute Humanity's karma.

When we say *Humanity's karma*, that encompasses all that lies in the shadows, for that is greed, incest, even murders. That is everything—killing each other, killing animals, killing plants and trees—it encompasses everything. When Humanity destroys something, when it destroys the sea-world especially, since the sea was their beginnings on this planet, to be part of the people who kill the dolphins for food, or to kill the whales for their oil, all of this is tremendous karma. That is part of Humanity's karma—the 75% that I am talking about, for when we were in physical bodies, even Yeshua and I were responsible for Humanity's karma. We could only do our part while in the body—think as purely as we could; be as kind as we could; and hope in that way it transmutes the karma of others.

The Goddess energy was sadly lacking in the days that Yeshua and I walked the Earth. We had, of course, the Divine Mother Mary; we had beautiful women in the Biblical crowd. We had Anna, Yeshua's grandmother, for example. We had the Essenes who taught the essence of spirituality and the importance of the Goddess energy. They taught this to the men in the Essene community also. Consequently, when Yeshua had his formative years in the community, he was being taught these different teachings. Remember, he too needed to awaken, for this was before he was baptized and before his full awakening came. He came from the sea. Therefore, the water of baptism had a great influence upon him. It brought consciousness at such a depth and rushed in so rapidly that it did throw him off balance and he had to go off by himself and rebalance.

Think how it would be in today's life. You now have psychologists, psychotherapists and spiritual leaders that you can turn to. But in Antiquity, who did you turn to when you knew more than they did? You would have these spiritual awakenings that flooded you, but you instinctively knew that no one else had them yet, for you brought them with you. That is what you are doing; that is what Yeshua and I were doing. That is how your DNA changed, for we were bringing a level of remembrance, a level of consciousness to the bodies.

Keep in mind, dear Readers that we were not perfect in every way. Just as you now do your best, we did our best. But it was not perfect. We were in 3rd dimensional bodies and, as you know as you sit in your 3rd dimensional bodies, we are not perfect at that time. They had to be programmed. They had to be revitalized. Even our food was not always correct for that time, for each body is different. One cannot feed a body exactly as one would feed another body. Each body has its own requirements for its nutrients. Some bodies required more fruit while other bodies could not take that much fruit for they would be in what you call your *water closet* for long periods of time. Each body is different. Therefore, the diets of bodies have to be different—to try and conform and to have everyone eat the same and the same amount is really rather foolish. It does not happen; it did not happen and it will not happen.

Even in your future as you get away more from eating animals and sweets and things of that nature and drinking coffee that has been cursed (*The coffee bean was cursed many years ago, so that with every cup of coffee you drink you are ingesting the negative energy of the curse. Saying a prayer or blessing over your coffee will transmute the curse.)*, you still will find that your diet will be varied compared to your neighbors or even to your siblings.

This Channel has a dear 6 year old grandson who as a toddler would not eat anything green-colored. Now where did that come from? It sounds very amusing to have a little boy pick peas off his plate because they are green; string beans because they are green; lettuce because it is green. Now doesn't that show you that he came from a different star system or a different planet? It is amusing, is it not?

Now dear friends, do you see the point I am trying to make as I went hither and yon? The Goddess energy will not be the same for everyone. Men must carry the Goddess energy, but it will not be the same for everyone. We have written on homosexuality. It was the Lord Kuthumi-Agrippa who wrote about the homosexual planets *(Book 7, Chapter 5.)* that one can go to in order to learn about the different energies and how people must experience that energy in order to finally bring the balance of the masculine and feminine principals within them.

It is a difficult concept for people—mainly for men, for some of your more Earth-bound athletes, we shall say, abhor any thought that they might carry a Goddess energy. But you see, dear friends, it is mainly semantics. They do not understand. We are talking about *principals* here. We are not speaking of personalities.

We also are speaking about the process of learning; the process of delving into your backgrounds; the process of analyzing your own thoughts—mulling over as to why did you do that or why did you do this; mulling over *what does this mean*? When I have incapacitated my body in some way, what was the purpose of that? What was the reason for that? You see that many of your male friends do not think in those terms. They do not realize that they created that. Why did they create that? Yes, it was a very physical sport but they still created that injury. What was that injury for? Men are not apt to think like that, are they?

It takes guts; it takes courage to sit and dwell on things of that nature—why did I create this? What was it about me that I created this? What was the lesson I had to learn? Why did fear and doubt settle into my back and break it? The thoughts were that strong. Why did I create that? Now I have to live with the pain for several months. Why did I create that?

As you sit with your pain, not able to do much, you think about that esoteric teaching. Why did I create that? It was a lesson was it not—how your thoughts create reality; how your thoughts can be so powerful that they can actually injure your body. How your thoughts can be so powerful and the manifestation is so quick these days that it instantly manifested in the Now instead of the next lifetime, as you walk around with a *bad back*, as you put it. It is instant manifestation of your thoughts, dear friends—a very powerful lesson. Whenever you start to think along that nature of your doubts and fears—*you cannot do this; you do not want to do this*—that is the time when you quickly negate that thought, transmute that. *Cancel, cancel, Back (referring to my broken vertebra)!* You cancel the thought before it can manifest so quickly. In other words, your lessons are no longer put aside for the next lifetime. They are coming one after the other, right on top of each other, getting your attention.

For those of you who do not pay that much attention to your body, your body will certainly tell you when something is off and you are not in balance. Think about this. Is not every illness in the throat chakra? Are broken vertebrae not in the third power chakra? It radiates forth. So, my children, watch your thoughts; be in your heart; watch the balance of your masculine and feminine principals. Are they balanced? Which one is dominate? For it is all important now—all important.

I AM Mary Magdalene. I will be back again within the pages of this book. Adieu.

(Thank you, Mary.)

You are welcome, dear one; you are welcome.

All right, my dear one, that was my Mary. We will call it a day for now and I will speak to you tomorrow when I come through Cynthia. (Yeshua/ Cynthia Williams teach a group at my house once per month.) 3-20-10

Again dear one, good morning, I AM Yeshua and I am returning to proceed with our book. I believe that you have sent 15 pages to our dear friend Heather to edit, and yet the Introduction is not quite finished. So let us continue with that and then we will change the theme somewhat and go to the first chapter.

We have been talking about the masculine and feminine energies and how important it is for that to be balanced in people's lives. I want to reiterate, dear Readers that this does not remain constant, but it is something that you need to be aware of daily. This Channel has a balance of the two principals, but there are times when she has one more dominant than the other. Therefore, keep in mind that they can change. It is like your aura. It fluctuates—the ebb and the flow. It is the same way with the principals. They are not always just balanced perfectly. Whatever the environment is will influence them so that one may be more dominant than the other. It is just the way it works.

We have another Being who will speak. He will be the last one and then we will move right to the chapters. So without anything more from me, I will step aside and let him introduce himself.

Good morning, Readers, **I AM Saint Germain.** *(Oh, Saint Germain, how good it is to hear from you again!)* Thank you my dear, I am always here whether you know it or not. (*Chuckles.*) But I did so want to be a part of your book—what could be your last book (?). Now you know we are going to be writing another one—co-authored—with our dear sister, Cynthia Williams, but for you personally, this will most likely be the last one. We hope to start the collaborated book in June.

Now as Yeshua was saying, the principals do not always stay balanced in one position, we'll say. They can move around. In other words, if you are in a situation where you really need to use masculine energy, that energy will come forward and dominate that period in your life. However, if you are in the feminine part of yourself, say a cooking class or decorating your house, you have brought the feminine principal forward and would use that in the more dominant position. Remember when you have finished your task and have cleaned yourself out and adjusted your energies, always make sure you have adjusted the masculine and feminine energies into balance also.

All you need to do is just set the *intent* that you wish these principals to be in balance. I do not believe that people are that aware of the fact that intent plays such a part in your life. All you have to do is make the intent that these are going to come into balance and it will do so, for you are now aware and that brings you into balance.

Today I wish to talk about a little different aspect of these two principals. There has been so much publicity about the homosexual gay community. The information is not always correct. People seem to think that when you are gay you are not using any of the masculine principal and that is not true. It just seems like that for one principal is more dominant than the other. The gay male will be more dominant in his feminine principal and the lesbian woman will be more dominant in her masculine role.

However, it is because that person is searching and studying the different effects and repercussions of being in that more dominant mode. Keep in mind that one does not just stay static in one principal but will still bounce around and use the other principal.

In this day and age there is so much prejudice against anyone who is coming out of the closet. That person is being **prodded**; that **person fears the purpose** of his or her life—to be a homosexual. That person came in to do that particular vocation, to be a lawyer or to be an interior decorator and to be gay. That is the person's purpose. Again there is so much prejudice against those choices. People who judge you really do not have all the mitigating circumstances. They do not know what your soul's contract is; they do not know this.

Sometimes, which is even more shocking, one will find that people who have decided on one principal or another as the dominant feature of him or herself will have a midlife crisis, and they will find all of a sudden that they are now bi-sexual. That is all part of it; that is the ending of the game. You have reversed the play. Say that you came in as bisexual and then toward the midlife crisis you decide you are a lesbian or are gay. Therefore, you divorce your spouse or if not married, you are more attracted to the same sex. It is all part of ending cycle with the game of homosexuality. It is a learning experience that souls take on—a powerful lesson. Therefore, that explains why so many times Daddy is no longer married to your mother but now lives with "Uncle" Bob. Or Mama is no longer married to your father but now lives with "Aunt" Jane. It is the ending of cycle or the beginning of a new cycle.

People need to have more tolerance about these kinds of situations. Surprisingly, when I walked your Earth and was associated with many of the royal families, homosexuality seemed to be more accepted. You had some of the young royals who were very feminine looking in their dress; they covered themselves with jewels and furs and pranced around mimicking the walk of women. It was more acceptable. They were not always in a closet as they are now in this present time period.

There is little more that one can say about the masculine and feminine principals. The idea must be approached that we are speaking of energy here. We are not speaking of just a whim, but it is an energy flow—an actual energy. Unfortunately, Humanity is not all that conscious that all is energy. They will look at a chair and note it is a solid maple chair. They do not realize that the chair carries energy of the maple tree.

As people advance in consciousness, they then become aware that everything **is** energy; that everything is One in this Universe. However, it will take a long time before people will accept the fact that homosexuals are expressing their contracts, going about their purpose, learning lessons in how to use this energy that they were interested in during this lifetime.

All right, dear Readers, I think that about does it for me, and I thank you so much for listening to me as we put the last cap on this Introduction chapter. I will step back now so that Yeshua may come forward and take over.

(Thank you Saint Germain.)

You are welcome; it is good to be back, although I have never gone anywhere—just to speak was good for me too. Thank you, I AM Saint Germain.

All right dear one that was our friend Saint Germain getting his two cents in, although you know it was much more than that (chuckles). Now I will say that the Introduction chapter is finished.

The book will have different features to it. It will have just one theme all through it, although the two principals will be frequently mentioned. The masculine and feminine principals weave their energy through everything and everything is in balance. You see in Nature, everything is in balance. It is Man that brings it out of balance by killing so many whales or dolphins. Man cuts down too many trees and that brings it out of balance. Remember that God had everything in balance until humans came onto the planet in whatever way, whether by space ship, the Ethers or the sea. It was Man that brought the imbalances.

We will close for now and meet again in Chapter 1.

I AM Yeshua

1 - COUNTERBALANCE

I AM Yeshua, also known as **Jesus the Christ**. As we approach the Easter festivities, shall we say, people remember me going to the cross, being crucified, being put into the tomb, and when Mary Magdalene came to look for me, the tomb was empty. I had risen. Later I say to her, *do not touch me for I have yet to rise to my Father.*

These are all concepts that the scribes wrote. Not all of it is true, as you have been told. If you can believe about different aspects, if you can believe in holograms, then you will know that there was a part of me that went to the cross and a part of me that did not. God has said in His book, *And Then God Said...Then I said...Then He Said* (*pg.30.*) (*Go to* www.awakenedhearts.com; or, www.godumentary.com *to order His book*) that I did not die on the cross. And yet people still believe that that happened. I can say that my life did **not** expire on the cross!

There **was** a person on the cross, but it was a **holographic image** of me. The person looked and felt by touch that it was real. However, it was a hologram of me. I did not die on the cross. And yet that story persists and even more so as we come into Easter time, the celebration (*of my victory over death*). This Channel is confused at times also, for she has heard and read so many stories concerning my death. Suffice to say that I still live and still walk your planet when I wish to.

Therefore, Readers, you have your work cut out for you, for you will have your belief systems stretched. You have certain ideas about your particular religious sect that has been given to you. You tend to hang on to those. Whereas I am telling you that not all of that is truth.

Now I am telling you that I came from the sea (*chuckles*) and that I was a Dolphin and that I was a Merman. Consequently, you will see how your belief systems will be stretched and how you must be open to change.

History is noted for giving forth a particular idea. People buy into that. Take the United States in the present time of 2010. History is being made every day about this government. And yet how much of it is truth? The public is given very little truth from the television, radio, and news papers. The truth is so…sometimes it is embellished; other times it is weakened. It is rarely **the** truth and nothing but **the** truth. So now you have history being made and 400 years from now people will read about the history of America and will wonder what is true. They will wonder if what they read is true and they will wonder if the history has been contaminated. I say it will not be total truth.

Therefore, when you look at history, know that you are not reading total truth. When you read your Bibles, know that it is not total truth. Consequently, when you read about the Crucifixion, know it is not the total truth! It is not. And yet the Fundamentalists refuse to change a single thought concerning me. It is not the total truth.

I have walked among you, whether you know it or not. I have walked among you, listened to you, listened to your discussions. It surprises me in that people sincerely want to know the truth but do not know where to go to capture it. If there has been enough said about a subject, they begin to question it. Did that really happen?

This government is struggling with the Health Care bill. Most of the Democrats voted for it; but none of the Republicans voted for it. How much of that is truth? How much of that bill actually will help the American people? Only time will tell, but you see what it did is that it kept President Obama's impetus going. It allowed him to now put forth other ideas. It gave him authority once again. Reporters speak about it in terms of a bank account—you have credit versus debit in your bank account. He now has more confidence; he now has credit in his bank account. (You realize that those are all metaphors.) That is all part of living history, is it not?

When you put the Bible into biblical history context, you can see where the Bible most likely is not reported correctly by the scribes. Some of the Bible was written 200-400 years after the fact. Therefore, you know that much has been made up. Those portions are not fact. And yet it is a beautiful book for it holds some truth. The story of Joseph and the Coat of Many Colors holds some truth.* There was a brother who was sold into slavery, but that was his contract. He did govern Egypt by the hand of Pharaoh. That was his contract. But as to the actual happening of Potaphar's wife wanting to compromise Joseph, that is very questionable, but it makes for an interesting story. Yes, Joseph did analyze people's dreams, but the examples that the Bible gives are questionable. There are many beautiful stories in the Bible, but that does not necessarily mean that they are truth.

Evangelists take any sentence or phrase in the Bible and they make it work for themselves in present time. Some do it more cleverly than others. It is quite amazing. It may not have been the meaning at all. The Disciples tried to convey my meaning, but they did not understand themselves. So how can you teach something you do not understand? When the 13th Apostle, Saint Paul, came around, he really distorted some of the passages. He had his own spin on them but paid dearly for it in the end—a martyr's death.

Have compassion for the characters in the Bible. There was something about them when they were acting upon their contracts. Even then they may not have remembered in order to really accurately give out the messages, for all of Humanity must remember first before they can go ahead and act upon their contracts.

As the souls go forth in physical bodies, they always go forth with a purpose for that lifetime and in that purpose are always the lessons that they must learn. Sometimes, you see, it takes several lifetimes to learn a particular lesson. In those lifetimes they would be repeating previous lifetimes, learning or attempting to learn. Invariably those lessons had to do with the balance of the masculine and feminine energies.

I do not think there is a single lifetime that one has had that has not carried that lesson. Is this the lesson where I will be using the masculine energy? Is this the lifetime I will be using more dominantly the feminine energy? This is always woven into your purposes. Many times it is at the end of your cycle that you finally realize and can name when you are using each principal. *Oh, yes that was my anima* or *animus,* as Carl Jung would name the energies.

Therefore, Readers, note where you are today; note what energy you are using. This Channel as she sits here recording my words, what energy is **she** using—intuitive, right-brain, feminine or the masculine left-brain? I will let you ponder on this.

All right, dear one, this will be it for today. I bless you dear ones, I AM Yeshua.

*(Thank you, Yeshua. *He was Joseph in that lifetime.)*

(Counterbalance, according to Webster: any force or influence that balances or offsets another.)

2 - A LITTLE THIS and THAT

Good morning dear Readers and to this Channel. A few days ago I, Yeshua, spoke about the Counterbalance that is also necessary when you are balancing your masculine and feminine energies. Counterbalance enhances energies. In today's work we will bring another Being forward. She is known throughout the world as the Divine Mother. So I will step aside now and let her title this second chapter.

Good morning everyone, **I AM Mother Mary—**at least that is what you call me. I have many names. Mary will do. In this book, the emphasis is on the two energies, the masculine and feminine principals. You have been told that you need to bring balance to those two energies. They need to co-exist. There will be times of course when you will use one in a more dominant way than the other.

When I was the Mother of your Lord, of course we did not know all of this consciously, but in many ways I was coming from the feminine aspect of myself. I was nurturing; I was being the Mother to my brood. And yet when decisions needed to be made, I could bring forth the masculine energy and shift gears and get into that way of being—that mode.

When we had to flee to Egypt because King Harrod was going to hunt down the Babe and kill it, it was the masculine principal we were using. We had to flee, so in that way the masculine mode protected us. The feminine energy would kick in as I nursed my child. It was many a long night that we felt unrest, a fear that we were being followed or that we would be found. We tried to blend in the best way that we could with people in that country.

Now in this day and age, people read the Bible and they wonder about the stories and they wonder about what is truth and what is not truth. We are all, **all** so delighted that this Channel and her dear sister, Cynthia Williams, will take on the project of bringing forth Yeshua's story. Cynthia is a superb direct-voice trance medium and Chako is a superb listener, channel, scribe, who always sees a project to the end. Her drive has never left her from her Saint Paul days.

I wish to speak about the glorious morning here in Arizona. For those of you who have never read Chako's books, she channels in an alcove in her bedroom that looks out on a large lemon tree that is currently full of lemons with some blossoms still. The quail go chirping by. I chuckle over the name of the town she lives in—Surprise. She has said *there is always a surprise in Surprise!*

Therefore, we are sitting now in this alcove. We are listening to the quail that always seem to be scurrying around for this bug or that bug, and the CD player is sending forth sounds from old hymns—no words, just the music. It is quite lovely. It provides a perfect background so that I might give forth what is on my mind today.

I believe I am in every book with the exception of her last one where she wrote about Saint Paul (*Paulus of Tarsus).* Life is a journey that can be exciting or it can be boring; it can be joyful or it can be sad. It has ebb and a flow to it. Many people blame God if a disaster strikes the family or if there is a serious illness. They buy into the ole time religion thinking that *God is punishing me* for something. People are so apt to think about being punished when they have created an illness. It is not punishment, dear ones; you are seeking a balance within yourself. Many of your illnesses happen because there is no balance. Life is a juggle. This Channel facilitated a grief group in Minneapolis, MN. Many of the participants thought their grief was a punishment of some kind. I hope you all realize by now that that is not so.

There are many reasons for a death as you know. Sometimes the soul is just plain tired of it all. It just wants to go Home and come back at a later time to start over, especially as we get closer to 2012. It is not unusual after someone has passed over to come back and kind of hang out with the family or a best friend. This Channel has an amusing story; while in her grief group there was an older gentleman. Every time she wanted to address him, she would address him by another name. He kept correcting her. So finally she said, *do you have a family member or friend by the name of…?* He said, No, not any longer … just died a little while ago. So she told the man that his friend is certainly still here because *whenever I try to find your name, I get his name!* And of course she had not even known his friend's name beforehand.

Therefore, you have these entities who may not want to let go. They are still attached to the memory of what it was like to be with you. They may be there to guide you, but most likely it is because they have not moved on. There are going to be a great many instances of that scenario playing out—souls who leave for they are just plain tired of it all, especially as living becomes more difficult.

Give yourself as much joy as you possibly can, whatever it is. Is it taking a walk or attending a sports game of some kind? Unfortunately, so much of Humanity thinks going to a bar is the place for enjoyment. They like that heavy energy; they feel at home there. Unfortunately, alcohol is not the answer. Alcohol is a curse actually. It deadens the senses. It helps you to forget, versus helping you process so that you can let something go.

In your lifetime you will fluctuate in using the two principals. You will find that you are more comfortable with one principal versus the other. However, as you get older you will realize that there must be a balance. You realize that you are using both, maybe for the same task.

People on the whole are so much more aware now than when I was in that Biblical crowd. People today seem to be more willing to change, to try new things. And yet there are some who will never walk a different path. I fear for the many Fundamentalists, for they are caught in that web. There is little truth but much dogma.

One of the fallacies Christians believe in is that Jesus will save them. *Come and love Jesus and you will be saved.* My son does not save anyone, but he can guide you to a fuller, more productive life. You see, the people give up old ways and come into—we'll say, *born again*—agreements. They may now be living healthier ways. They have given up their alcohol. They may have become better people. However, they equate that with Jesus saving them, whereas it is all of their own hard work! He merely is the Wayshower. Therefore, Evangelists, instead of saying *come to Jesus; he will save you*, need to say *come walk with Jesus for he is a Wayshower; he will show you the way to a more pure life.* There are so many fallacies concerning him.

We are so delighted that Yeshua finally will tell his story so that it can be published. That book will be a gem and a book that belongs in the school libraries; it belongs in the churches; it needs to be shouted from the

Evangelists' pulpits. We plan on having the book fan out across the world. It will be translated into different languages so the people, say in Germany, can read the truth once and for all. That is what Yeshua has in mind—*the truth, and nothing but the truth, so help me God.*

Name this chapter *A Little This and That.* I am speaking of this and that, aren't I? People, you will need to rev up your courage for the remainder of this year. You will need strength, not strength in muscle tone, although that will help too, but strength in the spiritual sense. You will need to look at your gifts, your virtues and see that they are brightly waiting for you.

It is the year 2010, where you will need much integrity, honesty, love, and caring—always love. The younger generation will still be thinking what they will do with their lives. Some will go to college and some will not. It is getting more difficult for parents to raise children. There is so much temptation for them—temptation to get on the Internet and delve into pornography; or get on the Internet and try to meet others that way. That is dangerous. There are so many predators waiting for the young innocent child.

Teenagers are dealing with their karma, much of which can overwhelm them, to the point where they decide *to heck with it* and get caught up into the drugs that are so available to them now. There are times, as their hormones are adjusting and there is rapid growth in the body, they may experience deep depression. In order to overcome the depression, they get hooked on the drugs, the uppers and downers.

I do not wish to say that they are unreachable at that time, but they sink so far into themselves that parents do not know what to do with them. Parents are apt to just throw up their hands or stick their heads in the sand. There are many teenage suicides these days. The soul just wants out. Life is harder than the soul thought it would be. Therefore, he or she takes his or her own life. Of course you know, suicide is the worst possible solution you could come up with.

Churches now are inadequate for teenagers, for teenagers recognize the fact that what is being taught to them is dogma and not truth. They rebel against having to go to church and listen to the same *boring sermon*, as they would put it. It is a difficult year for everyone—2010. And yet I cannot tell you that it will get better. Yeshua has said that this year is a lighter year and 2011 will be a dark year, but that could very well be in the eyes of the beholder; could it not?

My message for this morning is for all of you to look within; see what excess baggage you are carrying that you can let go of. It no longer serves you. Ask Archangel Michael to come forth and sever the cords. You do not want it anymore; you do not need it anymore. Let it go. Let those addictions go. They are not helping you. Change your outlook. Change your energy. Study your own virtues. It's your bank account. What do you have in your bank account?

One of the biggest and most productive acts you can do is to *forgive.* How many of you forgive yourself every day? Your body is your vehicle. The body elementals are helping you. Love your body; thank your body, even to the fact if you have evacuated your bowels in a wonderful purging, thank your body for the release of all the excess stuff that your body no longer needed. Thank it; thank it often; tell it you love it.

People forget that your body is a vehicle for you—your soul. The body will respond to you, act for you, fight for you if you care and love it in return. People abuse their bodies by staying up late at night, not giving it enough sleep, perhaps smoking, drinking coffee, and taking in too much caffeine. Do you not see how that is abusing your body? A body would enjoy a good night's sleep. A body would enjoy if you would stop smoking and let the lungs clear and heal. Your body is a vehicle that you had asked for, and it will work for you and be there for you. A body is a superb machine, a warm-blooded machine. Love it; care for it; feed it and listen to it.

If it wants a glass of lemonade versus a glass of iced coffee, choose the lemonade with the fresh lemons, sweetened with a little honey. It is much better for you than coffee that has been cursed.

I have spoken of different subjects this morning. I say *this and that.* We in the Heavenlies watch over you, listen to your prayers and answer when we're able to do so.

I love you, my children—children of God. I AM the Divine Mother.

(Thank you, Mother Mary.)

You are welcome, dear one. As I have said, this chapter is of this and that.

(But you spoke on several subjects, so that is good.)

Yes.

All right, dear one, shall we call it a day?

(Yes, thank you.)

All right, greetings.

3 - GOD COMMENTS

Easter Sunday, April 4, 2010, 10:00 AM. Good morning my precious Readers, ***I AM Yeshua****, speaking through this dear Channel of mine. I know there are so many different stories about me and the Easter experience—the empty tomb, the Ascension, crucifixion on Good Friday. Precious ones, truth needs to be told at last. I have promised Cynthia Williams who will channel me and Chako who will be my scribe and sit before me and question me, record me, watch the taping, that I will tell my story—the truth. She will be my right hand. She will be the one to form the book and get it to the publishers, for it is time. This will be an equal partnership between Cynthia and Chako, for one cannot do it without the other. One speaks and one types it up. One channels and one listens.*

However, this morning I am speaking from Chako's heart as we continue Book 9 which has a very important message for you Readers, having to do with the balancing of the masculine and feminine energies. As you have been told, you need to acknowledge that you have these two energies within you. They are not personalities; they are not egos; they are energies—energies, as in electricity. You have the masculine and feminine wires. They need to be there in order to have something work—light switches, etc. This is what your bodies are like. You have an electrical need inside of you—a flow. The water part of you, the sodium part of you, all help the electrical parts of you come together and flow correctly. One cannot function well without the other—the "masculine and feminine principals," we call them. These energies are so necessary and are all part of your enlightenment.

Those people in the third dimension (3D) who refuse to believe any of this and think the words I am saying are from woo-woo land need to know that they must awaken—remember who they are. They must remember. Did they take that life as a thief to learn a lesson? Did they take that life as a rapist to learn that lesson? While they are in prison, they will awaken or die from their lack of consciousness.

All must be addressed, dear ones. All must be addressed, remembered, so that you can rise to another dimension. You will never skip a dimension. The third will go to the fourth and the fourth will go to the fifth. Now I know it has been said on the Internet that you can go from the third to the fifth, and I say you cannot. So many of the Lightworkers are in the fourth right now but may not realize it.

It is easy to spot someone who is in the third dimension. You can tell by their actions—what are they doing with their lives? Now they may be very wealthy, but are they greedy? Do they give or do they give only because it can be taken off of their taxes? Do they have kindness or do they not? Are they so egotistical that they always think they are better than their neighbor? The foul language, the unhealthy choices for the television, the surfing on the Internet, going into the black corridors where the sexual thrill of a sexual predator lurks are all indicators of a 3D mentality—the third density.

The people in the fourth and into the fifth have a larger heart. They cannot bear to hurt anyone. Many times they must be reminded to give to themselves, for so many of them are apt to give to others before they give to themselves. People in 3D like to hurt others, like to kill. The fourth dimension (4D) is the transition. It is you awakening more. The fifth is all love.

Today for this next chapter, I wish to bring in One who has not spoken for a while. It is imperative that He speak now. I will step aside and let Him come forth.

Good morning to My children, **I AM** your **Father-Mother God.** I AM the Energy from the great Central Sun. I carry with Me many hats, shall We say. I have created this Universe; I have created this world. Now we are creating a newer world. I have been sending energies upon this planet so that all may raise their vibrations.

You know, Humanity tends to struggle so. It tends to make things harder than they are. It tends to make them so complex. Half the time that is why back in Antiquity, the people could not understand your Jesus because he knew how to keep it simple. Why embellish it? Why make something more complex? The fact that he spoke in simple parables...

They could not understand him. It made no sense to them. He spoke in parables so that it would trigger their intelligence; it would trigger who they were. So many of them were Masters and did not even know it; they were Masters who had come to experience that density.

This is Easter morning and the churches are full. The Pastors are delighted, for their coffers will be full. Churches are having a difficult time economically. People are not coming to church. However, on holidays, days such as this one, the churches are full. Little children, the girls, wear their new dresses. It used to be a few years ago, women would have new hats. There is much talk about the Easter bunny and the coloring of eggs—such beautiful festivities, remembering the Lord Jesus the Christ.

Many of the preachers will be telling and retelling of Jesus going to the cross and his crucifixion and then his rising from the dead. As he has said, he will tell his true story in a not too distant future. He will tell his true story of how he came onto the planet and what transpired.

I come this morning to give you My blessings, to give you My love. Many of you are dejected. You get caught up into the politics of the country. Since this Channel lives in Arizona, I am speaking of this country of America. Your president walks a fine line trying to bring enlightenment to his Congress. There are so many who fight him. They cannot see the purity of his heart. And yes, there are times when he makes decisions that others do not agree with. However, he is doing his best, and that is all anyone can ask for.

The remaining years leading up to 2012 will be years that will try many people. It is the breaking up of the duality, you see. Therefore, the dark part of the duality of Light and dark will be fighting to its last breath. This planet is no longer to be a planet of duality, Light **and** dark. It is to be a planet of Light and love and the sacred union of the Divine feminine and the Divine masculine—those two principals, those two parts of energy that I carry—Father-Mother God.

The energies will be difficult. This Channel was telling her daughter that when we experience periods of extreme weather *(two back to back blizzards in Washington D.C. area),* periods of earthquakes (*Haiti and Chile*), that most likely it is from man-made technology by the dark forces. (*See Matthew's Messages 3-29-2010 at www.matthewbooks.com)* As we come closer to 2012, severe weather and quakes will be intensified as the dark forces fight the Light in their last 3D gasp. They will do anything to disrupt the people of the planet at this time.

Consequently, everything will become more severe. Travel will become more difficult because of the weather, floods, mudslides, and just air travel will be difficult, dear children. It would behoove you to ask for protection, to ask for Me to come to your aid. You see, what I am talking about is free will. I cannot come and help unless you ask Me to because of your free will. I surround you with My love. I am always with you in your bodies whether you know it or not. I am just waiting for you to make the connection. I have come this morning wearing My hat of One who can channel to you all. Come to Me, dear children. There is that saying, I keep the Home fires burning; love is there and Home is waiting for you.

Happy Easter, dear ones, Happy Easter, I AM your Father-Mother God.

(Thank you, Father, thank you so much for the Easter blessing.)

You are welcome, My dear child. I am always with you.

All right, dear one, that was our Father.

(Mmmm, what a privilege.)

As it always is! All right, dear one, I give you my Easter blessings also. I AM Yeshua.

(Oh thank you, Lord. 10:25 Easter morning.)

4 - WARNINGS of THINGS to COME

Yeshua's *here and we are going to continue working on a chapter. It is about this time that we give this Channel, this scribe, the title to her book for she is always a little restless until she is given the title. We will now state the title:* The Masculine and Feminine Principals Are Balanced: The Goddess Returns to Earth. *You can sequence that in any way that you wish.*

I cannot impress upon you enough, dear Readers, the importance of this balancing act, and we'll say— the importance that your masculine, feminine principals, energies come into balance. Do not think you are one or the other. There will be times when one is more dominant than the other, but only for a short while. It is not meant to be in its entirety unless it is your homosexual game that you came in with for the soul's purpose and lessons.

Otherwise, for the heterosexual community, all must be in balance. And of course you have been told in previous chapters that you can use one energy more than the other at times during your daily life, but strive for balance. It is the balance that keeps the body healthy. When your energies are not in balance, then the illnesses happen. ***Illnesses are a sign of your body being out of balance****. Now I recognize there are times when it is most difficult to balance, especially when the body comes into contact with these strong man-made germs.*

The bronchitis germ sweeping the nation has disturbed the balance of many people. It is throughout the United States. It is at the point where I can state that 51% have endured this bug, had to go on antibiotics, have had it advancing into pneumonia with more antibiotics. That is just one germ that was created to upset humanity (and add to the coffers of the pharmaceutical companies). That germ will not be the only one, dear ones. You have had many such illnesses before.

Therefore, when the body does come into contact with these germs and cannot fight it for various reasons, you need to do everything in your power to bring balance again to the body. This Channel is one of those whose body was not at its height of being able to combat the different germs that are out there. She has been ill with this bronchitis germ for most of the month of March.

However, at the same time, she has been conscious of the fact that she could be contagious. She covers her mouth when she coughs. She washes her hands with antibiotic soaps frequently, especially when she comes home from being out in the public. You have a lesson in not spreading your germs among people; there is a lesson here that you need to keep foremost in your mind. When you are ill and need to go forth, take the precautions. Do not spit out on the street as so many men are apt to do. Cough into a tissue. Many people do not realize that they are contagious even if they are not running a fever. This is what I want to emphasize to you as we get closer to 2012. You need to keep this foremost in your minds. ***You may not have a fever, but you are still contagious—cover your mouth!*** *Any cough spreads the droplets of saliva into the air, and whoever is closest breathes that in and becomes ill.*

Today I will bring in another Being for the next chapter. I wish to bring our dear friend Saint Germain in, for he always has much to say. I will step aside now and let him proceed.

All right dear friends, I spoke to you in the Introduction. **I AM Saint Germain**. I come once again to write this fourth chapter. (I still have not named the chapter yet, so we will wait and I will give it to you at the end of my talk.)

As I was focusing on what to say—what would be apropos, what would be meaningful for you Readers—I was struck by the fact that so many people are concentrating on 2012. They know that that is the end of a cycle—or I will say that most of them know. The Lightworkers know, and even though they try to keep from going into fear, there is trepidation among Lightworkers. It takes a very strong person to keep faith and know that he or she will be in the right place at the right time.

You have been told repeatedly not to go into fear because the fear feeds into the fear of humanity. It is on an energy band; so any fear goes into that band and circles and circles the Earth and comes back to you with everyone else's fear a hundred fold. There is, of course, trepidation for people when they come to the unknown. There is fear in death. There is fear in going to the dentist. There is fear in hypodermic shots. Fear permeates much of your walk through life. It is one of the lessons. How can I walk my life without fear? You bring your faith. You bring your courage. You stay in your heart and you know—you have a knowingness—you know that all will be well with you.

You may not realize your purpose. You may not fully understand your lesson. But you will know deep down if you stay in your heart that you will be in the right place at the right time. Keep in mind, dear Readers, your free will and therefore, the angels, Masters, no one can help you in any way unless you ask for it. **You must ask for it**. Therefore, ask for that protection to come to you. Ask to be surrounded by the angels. Ask to be blessed by the energies of God. Do you realize that when we come to a person who is channeling, such as this one is, do you realize how fortunate we feel? The Channel was expressing her gratitude before this session—gratitude to be able to be of service for us, but dear Readers, put that in perspective. Put that into reverse and know how appreciative **we** are when someone such as yourself opens to be of service to us because you are giving us a gift. That gift multiplies for now we can give you our gifts.

Many times our gifts are symbolic. Many times our gifts are in the Etheric so that you will not reap these gifts maybe until you have left your physical body. Then you will be surprised at how many gifts are waiting for you in the ethers. It will be like Christmas all over again because you will be able to see them. You will be able to hear what was said once again.

Much of this will be done in front of monitors when you have your life's review. You will perceive all the dimensions. As you sit there you will see when you have been channeling, perhaps. You will be able to see the energies of a Being that comes to you. You will see the energies that are left behind when he or she leaves. You will see this and feel this and you will know that you were truly blessed. You will know that you in your way, by your willingness, by your cooperation, by your love, all of that blessed the Master that came to you. It is a two way street, Readers. It is two way. This Channel opens her heart in order to hear my words. She receives them and then in her diligence in her heart place that moves out so that I receive the appreciation. So you see the blessing is a two way street.

The Internet is full of Lightworkers' comments and teachings. Of course, common sense tells you that some Lightworkers are more advanced than others. Some have more to say than others. Some say it more accurately than others. They usually hold one theme and tell you how you are not alone in the different sensations that your body is going through as the Earth changes her vibration toward 2012.

I wish at this time to also reiterate that when you are reading these Internet articles or maybe scanning them as this Channel does that you will know, just know whether that message is for you or not—whether you resonate with it or not. Just because the person is a Lightworker does not mean you need to take everything in—his or her truth is now your truth. It may not be your truth. Therefore, dear Readers always discern. Do not take everything as verbatim and believe it, because even the best of channels do not always get it right for it comes through their energy system. If they are not clear, the information will not be clear or accurate—always discern.

With books—some people like our books and others do not. Some people read these books while many do not. Each person is growing and developing in his or her own way. The time will come when stories, articles on the Internet, will not be easily accessed. The Internet is going to have some growing pains.

Do you not see that while the Earth is being bombarded with energies, solar flares, or anything of that nature, that it will disrupt communication? It is better for you to not rely so much on the Internet. Do not rely so much on the television. It is time to let those machines rest a while. It is time for you to trust yourself—to listen to you. Then you will know what it is you need to do, where you need to go.

There will be difficult times coming. You have been told that. Ask for added protection. Stay in your heart. Be discerning. Use common sense. Change your patterns so that you are not doing something in a ritualistic way. If you walk some place at a certain hour, change the hour and walk in a different direction.

As the year 2012 gets closer to you, you could be under what we call a *psychic attack*. The dark energies will go after the Lightworkers. You could feel like you have been pushed as you fall down some place—anything to stop you for a while, to stop the Light for a while. That is the reason that the dark ones will be attacking more often. Ask for protection, dear ones, even in your dream state before you go to sleep, ask for protection in the dream world.

That is all that I wish to say at this point. It is not a very lively chapter, is it *(chuckles)*? Let us call this chapter *Warnings of Things to Come*. We have talked about discerning on the Internet; I have talked about discerning on your television; I have talked about changing your habits and patterns in your daily lives; I have talked about the trepidation that Lightworkers feel. I will say it again, stay in your sacred heart, ask for blessings, and ask for protection. All will be well. Know that and believe that—that you will be led; you will be at the right place at the right time and **all will be well**, dear ones.

I AM Saint Germain and I give you my blessings.

(*Thank you, Lord.*)

You are welcome, dear soul, and I know you have had a rough March. Your body could not fight the germ that you walked into. You have rested; you have kept going and your body is stronger now. All is well. Blessings, dear one.

(*Thank you.*)

All right, dear one, that is it for today. Greetings.

5 - NADA'S VIEWS on the BALANCE of ENERGIES

Good morning precious ones, I AM Yeshua. This book is coming along nicely. I do not have much else to say right now, so let us bring in the next Presenter. You will know her; you will know her well. I will let her introduce herself.

Good morning, my precious sister, **I AM Lady Nada**. (*Oh hello, Lady Nada.*) It is getting to be that I always come and speak to your Readers in your books. This book is about the balancing of the Feminine and Masculine energies. We say it in each chapter, but we say it differently each time in hopes that if the Readers did not get the concept in one way, he or she would understand it in another way.

You have been told that we are talking about energies, an electrical type of energy where there must always be two in order to make the whole. That is what we are talking about. Your body is not one **or** the other energies. There are always two in order to make the whole, the Father-Mother God, you see—masculine and feminine energies, masculine and Goddess energies, Father-Mother. This is what happens with your bodies. You can think of it in terms of the father-mother part of you—not your parents, but **you**. Are you not the parents of your body? They are not your biological parents but are you not parenting your vehicle that has been loaned to you even though it comes from the Earth? You still can say that that was replicated, that was created solely for you, solely for your soul's development. Each soul needs a body in order to develop certain attributes, certain virtues to regain consciousness on the returning to the original flame of Mother-Father God.

Let us name this Chapter 9, *Nada's Views on the Balance of Energies.* Yes, I like that. Yeshua has been teaching in many places throughout Arizona. He teaches about the importance of the balancing of these two energies and how this must be balanced in order for you to make your Ascension. Everyone who has ascended—every Master who has ascended—has balanced those two energies, the Masculine and Feminine energies. Otherwise, they could not have ascended.

Now, of course, you choose the sex of your body (*before you are born*). Yeshua was in a male form in his Jesus life. But never forget that he has had many different forms. He had to learn about many energies, just as all of you have had to. In his future book that will be collaborated by this Channel and Cynthia Williams, I will let him tell his story through them. But for now, know and remember, were you not everything on the planet? Did you not have a life, we shall say, as a frog? Did you not have a life as a wolf, a bear learning those animal energies—even a rock? Then there are the sea creatures. Did you not swim as a dolphin; swim as a whale or (*sun yourself as a merman/mermaid)*? There are even some who chose to be an octopus. If you did these different variations of a life on this world, do you not think that your Lord Jesus did the same? Of course he did; of course he did.

Why do you think that he and you chose all of those different ways of living on this world? How could one evolve emotionally, consciously, without knowing one's environment? You come to this world such as this Earth was—this aquatic world, as we have said in previous chapters—a water world. You came to experience this, all of it. As the world started showing land, you came upon the Earth again to experience that and to teach others. You wanted to know how an animal thinks; how a fish swims. Are they in schools of fish? Are they in pods like the dolphins—the different ways of living in the world? You wanted to know these things.

Then as you kept coming back—some think in terms of reincarnation—you kept coming back and chose different ways of learning, interpreting your environment, mineral (*rock*), plant (*tree*), animal (*dog*). You did it all. Now you see, dear souls, your time on Earth has come to the grand finale. You now have the choice of what you want to do next.

Do you want to ascend into the 5th dimension where all is love and from there go on and seek the adventures from other planets? Or do you wish to come back to this planet and live and enjoy the fruits of your labors as one of the Creators of bringing consciousness to the world? You have been told that the world will not stay the same. Its axis is off balance and it must regain its balance. When you picture a world with its axis off, would that not be similar to you as a human standing on one foot and not being able to get the other one down so that you are standing on two balanced feet? This all needs to be done; this all needs to happen to Earth.

Some of this sounds scary to people. They do not want to know what is *coming down the pike*, as the saying goes. They do not want to know what is coming, for it puts them into fear. Not everyone is eager to know the future. It brings up past lives where maybe their life was not that easy. Just in America one can go back a few hundred years to the *Salem Witch Hunt* era. Many of you Lightworkers were experiencing that terrible time. You were not allowed to be who you were. You were not allowed to speak your truth because the righteous priests were dictating how to pray, how you must have a certain relationship with God. They were telling you how to be, how to act, what to eat and when, what to wear. The control was very difficult for people. Amazingly enough it seemed as if the women were the ones who were scorned. It was the women who were dragged before the priests and called *witches*. Rarely did it happen to the men.

You see, many of those priests were wizards in their own right, but they were protected by the black cloak of the priesthood of the church. It was great hypocrisy in those days. Of course the Spanish Inquisition was also a time of dark energy.

Many of you have had lives in those dark periods of time because it was growth for the soul. You chose that; you chose to come into a body during those times for it was the experience, the knowledge, the wisdom and therefore, the growth for the soul.

Even if you had a life where you thought you had failed because you succumbed to the dark, when you passed over you learned there had been great wisdom in that life; you had learned a great deal. When you came back again, you had the wisdom then and the strength to fight the dark so that you did not play that out more than once. Most of you learned and were able to climb the next rung of the ladder.

There are so many of you in a transition period right now. There are so many of you struggling with *do I really want to ascend; do I want to do all of this inner work?* But you see, dear ones, you are coming from your 3rd dimension mentality. Yes, I know many of you are in the 4th dimension now, but when you do not wish to go forward into the 5th, are you not in those lower mentalities? You do not need to stay in that one spot. You do not need to play those games over and over again—the karmic wheel that never stops. You do not need to do that.

However, your consciousness gets stuck, shall we say, in that 3rd dimensional way of being, so that when you have your lifetime, you do not think of the fact that you are creating your life, that you are making choices that will actually draw you into further choices for better or for worse. However, they are still your choices and therefore, they are still your creations.

Humanity tends to get caught up in the latest gadgets, shall we say. The cell phones right now are rampant and they do all kinds of things, leaving the seniors in the dust because the seniors no longer understand the new technology. Therefore, many seniors are sort of just throwing up their hands saying *I want out of here; I can't take this any longer; I don't understand this generation—computers and cell phones—and when I no longer understand something, I am no longer learning it.* The result is *why don't I just get the hell out of here?*

Now that may seem kind of strong, but a lot of souls are talking just like that. *Why don't I just get the hell out of here?* Then they will create some kind of illness or some kind of accident that will happen simply because they have put this out into the Universe as a thought-form and the Universe and the Law of Attraction are giving that creation to them. They have put out that wish and their wish has been answered. Therefore, they will pass over. This will happen for many people.

We are into the spring of 2010, April, and you may think in some ways that not much has happened to America for the first four months. Congress still is bickering back and forth with the Republicans trying to beat the Democrats and the Democrats trying to stand firm. President Obama is juggling, *to make nice* with everyone. But he is fighting a losing battle for he is never going to be accepted fully, which is all part of his learning experience. Never forget that people in these high places who make decisions for hundreds and millions of people have their own set of karma that they are working, their own soul's purpose they are working on.

Your President Obama brought in his purposes, his work also. His purpose **was** to be President of the United States. Some Republicans may abhor that statement. Your Senator John McCain, a proud man whose purpose was being able to go to war, become a prisoner and to withstand torture, to learn that mentality, which he did, is basically a good man, but in some ways he has what psychologists call an *arrested development.*

That happened when he was a prisoner during the Viet Nam war; he was a prisoner of war. Many of your veterans have that *arrested development*, that time period in their life where time seems to stop for them and all they are is in survival mode.

There is great learning and wisdom in that mode, but psychologically they are very wounded and may be damaged beyond repair, shall we say. Your Senator McCain wants so badly to be President. However, you have a saying; *it is not in his stars to become President.* He has already proven and fulfilled his purpose from prisoner of war to Senator and there it will end. He has brought stability to the Republican Party but his ego wants more, for he feels by not becoming President he has failed. That is not true.

Every soul has a particular game plan. Some finish, or we will say accomplish, that game plan before others. Your Senator McCain is one of those people. Anything that he does now is more or less a joy or a pain for him as he creates his reality. However, he has come as far as he will in this lifetime. He has good genes as far as longevity is concerned. Therefore, his decision for the Ascension will be along the line of *I have completed my work,* the soul will say. And *it is time to go Home.* Many veterans will be thinking along the same line.

There are people in your own family who have lost touch with the present day and age, computers and cell phones. They are more or less just sitting in the sun, going through the motions of their last days on Earth, knowing they will soon be going Home. Meanwhile there are seniors who are getting what one might call a second life, a second chance to go up that ladder into Ascension. They are excited as to *what is next? What am I going to do next?*

The time has come, dear friends and dear Readers, to know where you are on your journey. Are you at the end and more or less just basking in the sun until it is time to leave? Or do you have many more years ahead of you even though you are in your senior years, many more years because you want to be a part of Earth's Ascension. You will ascend with her. It makes no difference if there are earthquakes happening around you. It makes no difference.

This Channel recently felt a part of Arizona sway for 30 seconds for she was feeling the earthquake in Baja California, the 7.2 quake (*4-04-10*). People in Arizona felt that. She knew it was not Arizona's quake. She thought to herself that California must be having a big one. And it did but with very little loss of life. Those types of quakes are really warnings, to awaken you, to get you prepared, for the Earth will rumble and shake.

Dear ones, that is all I wish to say for this chapter. It has been my privilege as usual to come and chat with you for just a while. Therefore, I thank you, dear ones; I thank you.

I am known as the Lady Nada, the consort of your Lord Sananda. Adieu.

(*Thank you Lady, it was nice to hear you again.)*

You are welcome, dear sister, you are welcome.

All right, dear one, that's another chapter under your belt. Have a good day; you have a lot to type up.

(Author: Sananda is the higher aspect of Yeshua/Jesus.
Lady Nada is the higher aspect of Mary Magdalene.)

6 - WORDS by KUTHUMI-AGRIPPA

Yeshua: *Good morning, precious one, are you ready to go to work? (Yes, thank you, Chapter 6 coming up.) It has come to our attention, as we are stressing the importance for Humanity to balance the masculine and feminine principals—that electrical energy—that some people are already doing it—their own higher selves are working diligently. But there are so many more people who need to do this.*

The Lightworkers, as you have been told, bring people up with them as they ascend. However, people need to know this in a conscious way—this knowing that this is one of the criterion that needs to happen. We stress this in our books, but oh, how we wish—and I am a blend this morning—but oh, how we wish that the pastors, priests, and rabbis would talk about this in their morning services, or in their afternoon or evening services. Wouldn't that be wonderful? So many people do not have a clue as to these inner workings of their body. Physically or spiritually, they have no clue.

Therefore, dearest ones, we keep stressing this in the chapters, do we not? As the Lady Nada was saying, each chapter brings it to the Readers' attention in different ways—the importance of the balancing of your energies. Not everyone, of course, remains balanced, for they will tune into one energy or the other throughout their daily lives. However, at night, if you could make it part of your nighttime ritual as you go about brushing your teeth and washing your face, think at the same time, or just give a prayer to your angels, or the Father or your higher self: Bring me into balance; bring me into alignment. *Of course, it always helps to say please and thank you.*

This morning, this Channel got up bright and early (in order to channel). We will be bringing in another speaker for Chapter 6. You have caught on, I am sure, as Readers of these books, that this is how we set our books up. We have a theme and then we bring forth different Masters who wish to speak on a certain subject. They do it with such pleasure, and we have often joked and chuckled how they actually line up, for they are so eager to speak. To all of you who channel and to all of you who do not realize that you can channel, it is such a privilege for us to come to you. If you only knew how much we Masters love to come forth and speak what you might say is our two cents' worth. But I think you would agree that you could think in terms of two cents being two beautiful gold coins.

Now let me step back so that the next one in line can step forth. We have just had a beautiful woman's energy in Chapter 5, so let us now have a male energy. You will recognize him. I will step back now and he will come forth.

Good morning to our Readers. It is such a pleasure to come once again. I have a new name, but you know me as Kuthumi, Master Kuthumi. However, I went to my retreat (*for a time)* and I was in solitude and I basked in the energies of our Father. I was given a new title. **I AM** now **Kuthumi-Agrippa**; or as my title states, **King Kuthumi-Agrippa**, the **King of Love and Wisdom**. That is such an honor. The energies are beyond description. I am filled with them. I no longer am the same person. Therefore, I come forth in order to give you a new flavor of me, and while I am speaking, this Channel is filled with my energy. (*Thank you, Lord.*) And the energy will be in this book—*love* and *wisdom*. It is a potent combination, is it not?

The theme of this book is about the masculine and feminine energies. Carl Jung, the Jungian psychologist, called them the *animus* and the *anima*. He was correct in his perception. Therefore, for those of you who have a more intellectual bent, go to the psychology section in your library and read up on his theory. He had much to say about those two principals. He may not have coached them in the terms we use today, but you will get an excellent lesson in his teachings. It might help you to understand more.

This Channel, since her degrees are in psychology and transpersonal psychology, felt right at home and knew right away the concept of the masculine and feminine principals from Carl Jung's teachings.

Every thing you do, every task you accomplish, dear Readers, you have used one or the other of the electrical principals and probably have not given it that much thought. You just did your task and did not say *OK I must bring my masculine principal forward in order to use my hammer on this nail.* The Feminists would say *but we can do that too*—and that is true, but that would be the blending, would it not? That is the balance, for the masculine and feminine energies both would be hammering the nail. Isn't that a good balance?

It is not desirable for the homosexual community to feel they are one or the other—male and using only the female energies. Or female and using only the male energies. That is not the correct way. There needs to be a balance, you see. Even though you are in a body that prefers a similar sexual orientation, you can still have a balance of those energies. You need not be so slanted to one or the other. However, that probably is for the future, for some of the male bodies can be so effeminate and a female body can be so macho. Of course, they are learning their lessons; of course, they are learning what the soul brought in to experience. However, even they need to balance.

As you make your Ascension, you will not do so unless you are balanced. Now, many times your soul and higher selves are working furiously behind the scenes, shall we say. They know what needs to be done. They work bringing past lives forward so that you will have the experience, so that you will have the opportunity to transmute the energy. You will have the opportunity to say *cancel, cancel, cancel* and flip that negative thought into the positive. Those are all opportunities that the souls give you so that you can address the particular energy that you were feeling—angry or sad, etc.—you can address those energies and bring a positive nature to them.

This morning as I look over your world—and we Masters can do that—to see the discord that is happening, we can see the sparks of Light. We can see wars; we can see the people being blown up in the war zones. If you get high enough up in the atmosphere and look down, you have a broader perspective as to what is on the horizon, do you not? We can see how people fight to be balanced. Is that not the goal of everyone, whether they know it or not? Isn't that getting to be a common observation people make? *I just feel out of balance.* It is very real to them, and they probably are out of balance.

If you are coming from greed or inappropriate anger, are you not out of balance? If you are in fear, are you not out of balance? When you are balanced and in alignment, there is no fear; there is no anger. There is peace when you call upon it. Peace. There is balance in peace. Many times people need to search for a particular place to go to whether it is inward or outward, whether you go to the beach to walk along the shore in order to find peace.

This Channel used to walk the beach when she lived in California. She went to the beach after classes in graduate school. She walked the beach and sang, yelled, and shouted, knowing that she was clearing energies within her. Then after about an hour, she would get back into her car and drive the long commute home. Therefore, you see, she was able to bring peace and a newer revitalized energy after a day or several days of classes and long hours of listening to lectures.

The areas of the oceans hold such healing energies for people. However, as you have been told, now is not the time to be living on the coasts, for the Earth must go through her growing pains and she must become balanced. As Lady Nada was saying, the Earth axis is off. It is similar to standing on one leg like a heron. You must put the other leg down and balance.

Dear Readers, if you would bring in more joy to your life and use more laughter and not be so serious, if you could turn off your judgment button, if you could stay in your heart, that sacred heart which is in back of your regular heart chakra—you enter in between the shoulder blades—if you could do that, you would find yourself moving more into balance.

And as this Channel does, you can command every cell, molecule, electron, atom in your body to come into perfect alignment according to your Divine blueprint. Just say that as a mantra; say that several times a day. Let it become automatic for you to command everything in your body. It will obey. That is how it has been created. It is a machine in some sense, but it is a loving flesh and blood creation. But you are the parent and you guide it and love it and do right by it.

You make your thoughts more pure. You eat more that your body is craving of the good stuff—fruits and vegetables. You can drink the green juice found in your stores that has copious amounts of chlorophyll from the green vegetables and the fruits used to sweeten it, like kiwis. If you can do these things, you will find that you can come into balance. You will heal more quickly.

You have been told that coffee has been cursed—the coffee bean—so it would be wise to not drink coffee. It would be wise of you to limit your tea and perhaps drink green tea which has a more healthy aspect instead. Watch what you put into your body, Readers. It is so important at this time.

Let us name this chapter, *Words by Kuthumi-Agrippa*. I have said what I deemed to be important this morning. I have not talked specifically and technically in an academic way, but in a very simple, natural way that would not be offensive to any one, which would not reek of being in "la-la land." I have used just plain common sense. I have spoken in simple terms, common sense, wisdom, and coming from love.

Peace be to all of you, my Readers; it has been my pleasure. I AM Kuthumi-Agrippa, King of Love and Wisdom and I greet you.

(*Oh thank you Lord.*)

You are welcome, dearest one; you are welcome! You do a wonderful service with these books that are spreading out more and more into different countries. You do not give yourself enough –hmm, some people would raise an eyebrow if I said *praise*, so I will use a different word—you do not give yourself enough pats on the back for what you have accomplished. It is greater than you know or even suspect.

Good day, dear one, good day.

(*Thank you, Lord.*)

All right, dear one that was our friend Kuthumi-Agrippa. Those who wish to may read up on King Agrippa in the Bible. He was a great king, but I doubt if the scribes gave him full credit for that.

This is it for today, dear one, until we meet again.

I AM Yeshua.

(Thank you, Yeshua.)

You are welcome.

7 - AA MICHAEL'S INTERPETATION

*Good morning to one and all, **I AM Yeshua**, back again so that we may continue this book. I am very pleased. This scribe, this Author, was working diligently on it this morning because there are so many other files that need to be finished once we have completed our subject—Copyright page, list of previous books, bringing* About the Author *pages up to date, and so forth. It will be the seventh chapter this morning. There will be several more.*

I wish this morning to bring in another soul as we keep balancing back and forth the different masculine and feminine principals, energies, animus, anima and any other names you wish to call them. They are very important, and you need to be aware of them in your daily lives. I will step back now and let this great Being step forth. I then will come back for the closing words. (Thank you, Yeshua.)

Good morning everyone, **I AM Arch Angel Michael (AA Michael)**. *(Oh, Michael, I am so tickled that you came! I really was not expecting you to be next until just before you announced your name and I started chuckling with joy, for I knew it was you.)* Well, you know we love being a part of your books, so I would have come at one time or another before this book was finished. I am going to name this Chapter 7, *AA Michael's Interpretation.*

I recently was popping in and out of various channels—some you would recognize and others you would not, for I channel all over your world. This may seem to some of you Readers as *overkill* as you put it (*chuckling*), but actually, you see, different people, different cultures, different countries have a different take on life. Therefore, someone such as I needs to come forth and speak in ways that those in foreign lands might understand also. Not everything (*information*), you understand, can be sent out from America.

Therefore, I have talked all over the world (*on Ascension*) and repeatedly, or I will say I have *chewed my cabbage* more than twice over. It is important now, dear Readers. Time is of the essence. We are speaking of 2012.

Yeshua, in a gathering at this Author's house (4-18-10) and while I peeped over his shoulder, talked about **2017**. Now how many of you Readers have gone that far ahead in the future? We bring those future numbers to you in case any of you retain the old fear that the world is going to stop at 2012. I hope you realize that that is not true. Earth is merely *changing clothes*, we will say. She is merely shifting gears, getting ready to forge ahead. As Yeshua was implying, everyone would forge ahead to 2017 and beyond.

It is going to be a glorious time for you—1000 years of peace that the Bible speaks of. However, human nature being what it is, you will still have your squabbles between neighbors, even between your neighboring countries there will be friction, but there will be no disastrous wars. There will be peace in the sense as much as humanity can understand what peace is.

How many people experience peace that is beyond understanding? Not very many because your mind is rapidly tripping on, doing its thing while the heart yearns for peace. Many times people need to go on vacation or they need to go to the coast, the oceans, or go to the forest, anywhere to find peace. And yet those places are no longer peaceful, for the Earth is still making her transition. But dear friends, it will happen; it will happen.

I wonder how many of you realize you are preparing for your Ascension. I also wonder how many of you are preparing for your immortal bodies. How would you like to reach a certain age and then know you will no longer age beyond that? But you would start a regression of age, becoming younger.

This Channel recently had a dream where she was in the backseat of this huge car and it was speeding along very rapidly, but it was traveling in reverse. The gear was in reverse! She exclaimed to the driver who she did not recognize that they were traveling backwards and expressed her concern. He replied that yes, when a car was that large, one had to be very careful when reversing.

Now in dream symbols you know a car represents your body. Therefore, this dream symbolized for this Author that she actually was travelling backwards in time, reversing the cells of her body. Now since cells work rapidly, most the time that would mean everything was reversing rapidly in her body. She is a senior-senior at this point, and she will continue to advance emotionally, spiritually, intellectually, for she has a fine mind, but her body's age will be regressing splendidly.

At this point the above does not make all that much sense to her. How can you look at your body and see your hair that would be white if you did not trot yourself to the hairdresser once a month to have the chemicals put on your hair to make it blonde versus white? But then she is a woman and women are allowed to have some vanity as long as the vanity brings joy. If you are totally vain and that is all you think about—your appearance—then NO, that is too much. But if you want to change your hair style or change your hair color, why not? It is your body, as long as you are kind to it and your body accepts this. Why not be light brown or blonde instead of white? That is your choice. So we say, *hey, go for it, girl! (Chuckles)*

Last month at Chako's house, I came through Cynthia Williams and worked with a new person to this small group that Yeshua teaches once a month, and she was just learning how to channel. Therefore, I came through and gave the whole group a sense of me, just a minute fraction of who I am. However, it gave the group a sense of what I was like. It helped this Channel, for now she knows that when she channels me, it truly is Arch Angel Michael (AA Michael). I do enjoy coming through the different vehicles, or speaking over their shoulder, we'll say, in a telepathic way. I do enjoy it, Readers!

This Channel on February 17, 2010 gave a presentation on the book that she had written with the help of Yeshua. She titled the book *Paulus of Tarsus: A Man Driven by the Word*. I did not speak in that book. Why I am bringing it up is because there were so many people (*in the large group*) who had not heard the truth about Saint Paul, or *Paulus* as he is sometimes called, using his Roman name. They had not heard that he, even though the Vatican had pronounced him a saint, did not believe that he was worthy of sainthood.

He was in a third dimension body and he struggled with his own emotions. However, he gave all of himself to the task of bringing in Yeshua's word to the Gentiles and to anyone else who would listen. He is to be commended and not damned, for he never lost his purpose. Now he did step off the path once in a while and enjoyed a bit of power, but his drive to get the word out about the Lord Jesus Christ never faltered, never in all of those years in prison.

Why am I bringing all of this up? It is the importance of following your heart, the importance of staying out of your brain, your mind. It is only the instrument of your heart—this purpose, this drive the souls bring in. You have the drive through a female body or a male body. You have this drive continuously soaring through you—continuously. Then you have the choice. It is a subconscious choice, but it is a choice to come either from your masculine principal or the female principal. The masculine always needs to be tempered by the feminine and the feminine must have the balance of the masculine.

As you may know with this Ascension, it is primary that you are balanced in these two principals—no matter what your sexual orientation is, no matter what your body gender is—you need to be in balance.

I have gotten somewhat off track, but I wanted you to know the importance that this date of 2012 is for everyone, for it is the date of the grand Ascension. You will be walking through another door. You will be walking into a different dimension—4's going to 5D and 5's going to 6D and a smattering of 6D's going into the 7th. Dimensions are doorways and each one holds 12 levels that you must conquer; you must master before going on to the next one. Each dimension has its own properties. When you go into the 5th you leave the dregs; you leave the dross of the lower energies behind you. They are not even in your thought processes. You leave them behind you.

In a previous book, I talked about when I visited the various battlefields and watched the soldiers fight. If there were not so many dying, I would say it would be like watching a movie, similar to *Saving Private Ryan* (*with Tom Hanks*), knowing that everyone was playing his or her role. As the world moves into this 5th dimension, those terrible scenes, those terrible plays will stop, for all must rise; all must be transmuted. That is evolution.

I was telling you about this Channel presenting the *Paulus of Tarsus* book in February 2010, and how she struggles with channeling. It is a test for her for it is a test in trusting, trusting that she will hear the correct words. Now she will be collaborating on a book with that beautiful voice-channel, Cynthia Williams. We are so delighted; we are so excited, for Yeshua will tell of his lives beginning with his life on this planet. I do not know all of what he will say. But he needs to tell of his life, for there is getting to be too much distortion about him.

This Channel was voicing to Cynthia that she and Yeshua have written many books, this one being the ninth, and yet her information differs from what others say about him. Yeshua came forth and whispered into Cynthia's ear and gave her a mental picture that she shared with this Channel.

If someone is channeling a Light Being and that Light Being is describing a chair that she is standing in front of and the Being describes the arms of the chair and the front seat—it is like this and like that. She is given the full description. Then along comes Cynthia or someone else. Cynthia is given a different description of the same chair for she is standing in back of the chair—looking at the back of the arms, legs, head-rest. She is given the description of that view.

Now when they both walk around the chair do they not see that both descriptions are correct? This Channel, Chako, has received different comments that her information differs from others. But can you not see how this is not so? She and others are describing the same chair but from different views.

We could use another example—someone who has climbed Mt. Sinai, as this Channel has done. She had her perceptions. She knew how it was for her and what she saw. And yet someone at the same time could be climbing the Mountain from another angle, from the side or from the back, or being lowered in a helicopter. What would that description be? It would be entirely different than from Chako's. You could be lowered by helicopter and have an entirely different description.

Therefore, if all three people wrote a book and each one described the Mountain, would you say *No that is not the Mountain; I saw this. No, that is not the way it was; I did this.* Do you not see that the Mountain is still the Mountain? Therefore, dear Readers, as you read these books and then may read other books, always know there could be similar descriptions of the same event. *This is what happened during the crucifixion.* This is what happened and many have described it. This Channel has her own book—*Realities of the Crucifixion*—that has an entirely different slant on it, while other books may have a different version.

Therefore, Readers, use your discernment, but realize that there could be other descriptions that could be just as accurate. Leave an open mind.

That was the main subject actually that I wished to speak about. One needs to have an opened mind so that several descriptions of the same event can be allowed. We are talking about the Law of Allowance—that it can be allowed.

All right, dear Readers that is my message for today. We are speaking about the different principals keeping in balance, always in balance.

I AM the Arch Angel Michael and I greet you this morning. Greetings.

(*Thank you, thank you very much, that explanation was really needed.)*

Yes, it was (*chuckles*) and that is why we decided to do it. You see, Yeshua needed someone else to make that explanation since he is the one who had given you the information on the *Realities of the Crucifixion*. Then you hear different versions of what he has told other people. So this just states it for people that there are more ways to describe something, more than just one way. And all are truth in their own way.

(*Thank you.*)

You are welcome.

All right, dear one, you got the object of that chapter, I take it. (Yes, chuckles, *thank you, that clears it up for a lot of people, for I still hear from some questioning the material that seems to differ from what they had read or heard elsewhere.) I know, dear one, you have struggled over this for a long time and I hope this will alleviate some of that stress for you. Good day.*

8 - QUAN YIN'S OBSERVATIONS

Good morning to our Channel and our precious Readers, we are staying on top of this, and I hope you too are flipping from chapter to chapter and enjoying what we have to say. As we have told you, we do our best to make the energies masculine or feminine, even in the chapters. Therefore, since you have just heard from that wonderful androgynous Being, AA Michael—we'll say "it" is a "he"—and it is now time to hear from a woman. This Channel had already intuited that she would be our lovely Quan Yin. Therefore, I will step aside and let this Goddess of Compassion tell you what she wishes to speak about this morning.

Good morning once again to this wonderful group of people who are reading these books so avidly, **I AM** the **Goddess Quan Yin**. Since this book is about the Goddess energy, it is quite appropriate that I come forth this day to speak to you. Chapter after chapter, we—and I shall say "we" for I have been blended in with all of the other Presenters—we speak to you of the different energies, the masculine and feminine energies, do we not? And yet here I am in a woman's body and my main energy is compassion, the Goddess—the feminine. However, at the same time I am also balanced with the masculine. I just do not wear the male's suit of clothes, nor do I have a beard.

This Channel has been thinking about this because as you come closer to the Ascension, you will be rising to different dimensions. You may be a female and rise as a male or be a man and rise as a female. (*These teachings were given by Yeshua through voice-channel, Cynthia Williams, during his class 4-18-10.)* That is so confusing to people. However, I will let Yeshua explain that to you when the time is right.

When I was a little girl growing up, I was always treated as a female object, we'll say, for you know the Oriental culture reveres the female child if she is in a position to bring money into the family. So many times these precious little girls are sold as sex objects, for you see, if they are especially beautiful they can bring in much money which helps the poor family—the peasants, the farmers. Therefore, in that case the girl-child is looked upon with delight. In other words, you could look upon her as a bright penny or a gold piece.

Cultures in different countries and nations are interesting, are they not? You have all heard, I am sure, of the binding of the female child's feet. I have spoken about this in a previous book—again, all for the purpose of the sexual delights of the male person.

Therefore, why I am bringing this up is to alert you that when a woman—or we will start with the small girl-child—is made to feel special with a pretty dress and is primped according to that particular culture—whatever is allowed as to the making up of the face or the making up of the hair—all of this is done to entice the male.

However, what is happening to her principals inside of her? Is there not a predominance of the feminine energy then? Where has the masculine energy been allowed? It has not. So you see there are generations and generations in China where the energy is quite off balance within individuals.

Now so as not to leave the little girl-child as the only example, let us speak of the little boy-child. He is given schooling either from his parents or a school teacher to teach him how to be a man—to enjoy a man's privileges, which is of course highly sexually orientated.

That male principal is stressed so that the child will take on as much of the masculine ways of reacting as possible. This is what leads him to so much warring. If you are in your masculine energy all of the time, how do you handle anger? Well, back in those days in Japan, you could train as a Samurai and you could chop off someone's head if you were in anger.

If there is too much of the masculine principal, then it overpowers the person so that most of the negative emotions are emphasized. Think of many of the negative emotions: greed, terrible anger and rage, lies and thievery, coveting what does not belong to you. All of those negative emotions become exaggerated when there is a dominance of masculine energy.

Now I know with the female, when she has a dominance of her energy, she also can use the negative emotions. She can go into rages; she can go into extreme jealousy of another woman; she can be outrageously sexual, vying for men's attention.

Therefore, Readers, you see what can happen when one's energy is not in balance. Many of you can look back at your own lives and start to pinpoint when you were not in balance. And so often it happens right around puberty when your karma comes in and hits you. Up to that time you have no karma unless you have created some more. But around puberty, your karma comes in full blast—everything that you signed on for. Most of the time it is all too overpowering, and you are unable to bring balance to your body.

There is such a need to have this information taught in the schools. You would think, *would it not be wonderful if a young person were taught this right from the beginning about the different emotions—how to play fair; how to play with love and gratitude, how not to be the bully; how not to fall into jealousy.* If these things were only talked about—maybe even by your school counselors or during your health classes—*(to instruct the children about their energies, in order to help bring balance).*

I was from a privileged family, and therefore I had much of everything that I wanted given to me. Then when I went out into the world, it was not like that at all. I found myself in one situation after the other that required me to bring the depths of my soul forth, to be in my heart with compassion and to learn this repeatedly, being in continuous pain of grief, all to hone the virtue of compassion, all so that I could master this and earn the right to be called the *Compassionate One.*

It is a long task; everyone and whether you know it or not each of you has taken on a particular way of Being so that you will hold that virtue and be known as that. Your Mother Mary is known as the *Queen of Hearts, Queen of Heaven,* for she earned that title. Lord Jesus or Yeshua is known for his wisdom and his love and for his peace, forgiveness and for his healing—the *Great Physician* they call him. And yet he was able to touch your higher selves and knew that you did not have to have that illness or disease any longer. There could be instant healing.

Each one of you learns a trait and then you will have lifetimes of earning that. This Channel is from a medical background so the members of her family, her mother, father, and aunt and she have had lifetimes where they are in the medical field in some way. In this lifetime she chose the more spiritual path of psychology—transpersonal psychology.

Her mother (*Ethel Humphrys Priest, MD, 1892-1986*) chose public health and pediatrics, for she loved the babies and saw to their health care. She was very wise in that. In her town of Napa, California, she talked the dairy farmers into giving the poor people in town their skim milk instead of just slopping it to the pigs. In that way the children had milk. Of course we now say that dairy is not that good for you, but this was back in the depression days (*1930's*) and milk was good as far as being nutritious for the whole family. They may not have been able to buy steak, but they could have a free glass of skim milk.

Down through the years this has changed because now people have the convenience of fast foods. It is just easier for people to go into the fast food restaurant and have the hamburger, French fries, and the soda pop, which comes in two choices—loaded with sugar, or loaded with chemicals in order not to have sugar. There is much about nutrition that people have yet to learn.

There is a woman (*Sally LeSar*) in Indianapolis, Indiana, who teaches a spiritual energy class by phone. She brings forth many of the Masters that people are familiar with. It was AA Metatron and the Lord Melchizedek who told the students not to drink any brown liquids. Now that was rather a puzzle at first until one started thinking about the color of everything that one drank. Of course that is coffee, tea of any kind, and all the brown soda pops. In some way those liquids were not compatible with the energy work that was being done on the students' bodies. *(And you have already been told that coffee carries a curse.)* This falls into the category of keeping the body as healthy as one can as the energies are transmuted, transformed and re-arranged. One does not always need to know the *why* of it.

One does not need to know the full extent of the Masters' energy work. In fact AA Metatron brought through too much energy which caused the disconnect of the phone lines that were involved. He came back on a few minutes later and said he had assigned an angel to monitor the phone lines for him.

Therefore, Readers, be conscious of everything that you put into your mouth. Even soy milk is no longer good for you as it has been genetically altered. There is so much to teach you and so little time left. We are conscious of that. Consequently, we bring you what we can and hope you will meet us half way. When you have been told not to drink anything brown, it is hoped you will follow those suggestions. You need to polish up your trust when you are working with the higher Masters. You may not know all that they do, nor is there a need to know. It is just your mind wanting that information.

So my dear souls, I will conclude this chapter. Why don't we name this chapter *Quan Yin's Observations,* for I have spoken on many subjects? We try to make each subject interesting, but really the emphasis is on the masculine and feminine energies that need to be balanced. Even these books are helping you to get ready to go forward, to rise to that next dimension. You have 12 levels in each dimension, Reader, so there is a great deal of homework that needs to be done by your souls, your higher selves, who are working diligently behind the scenes, shall we say.

I give you my love and my compassion for all the work you have done and will be doing.

Until we meet again, dear souls, I AM Quan Yin.

(*Oh thank you, Quan Yin, that was lovely.*)

You are welcome, dear soul, you are welcome.

All right, dear one, that was our Lady, or we can say Ladies' Night with the female energy. There will be a few more Presenters coming forth and then we will start the Conclusion. This book will not be as long as the others, for there is just one thread running through it—the principals must balance.

Until next time, dear one, blessings.

(Thank you, Yeshua.)

9 - THE GENDER EQUATION

Greetings, precious ones, **I AM Yeshua.** I will be dictating the information this morning. I will name the chapter later on. Up to this point we have been talking relentlessly, you would say, about the importance of the masculine and feminine energies being balanced. It does not make any difference as to what gender you are, you carry both principals and they need to be balanced. However, on occasion throughout the day, you may be using one principal more over the other but then bring them back into balance. Keep them in balance when you go to bed and when you wake up in the morning. Just say *I wish to be in balance with the principals.* .

It is coming to the time when this Earth will be going through her graduation phases even more so. There will be times when you will question whether you have made a correct choice or not—whether to leave an area or to stay put. What I can say to that is *stay in your heart.* When you get confused, turn it over to me and the Father for clarification. Sit on it for awhile. It does not have to be instant, especially if your message is to move; it does not have to be instant. Go into your heart. Or for those of you, who have learned how to use a pendulum, swing your pendulum and trust it; trust that you will get the answers.

You have been told to stay away from the coasts, for there could be inundation of waters. This could be from tsunamis, or it could be from hurricanes. You have been told to stay in your heart and stay out of fear, for fear and other negative thoughts simply go out and hit the *Ring-Pass-Not*, the band of energy that does not allow negative energy to leave the planet, and then the negativity comes back to you again multiplied by everyone else's negative thoughts of the same caliber.

It is a time to not be afraid. It is a time to discern distortions that are in your media, the newspapers, television, and your movies, for even movies are not always up-lifting. Some movies are historical in nature and can be interesting (*Australia*), but each has had its growing pains. During all of this you are to keep asking yourself *am I balanced; am I in this principal or that principal; can I bring them into balance?*

I have told my little group that meets in this Channel's house once a month, although we may skip a month now and then, the importance of the balance of the masculine and feminine energies. I have told the group that when you ascend if you are a male you will ascend as a female body.* If you ascend and are a female you will ascend as a male body for you will be going back to what you may call your *roots.* But if you are millions of years old, you realize that that could be quite a journey.* (*See Appendix for his/Cynthia's teaching on this.*)

This Channel's soul is male; it is a male soul. Therefore, while she is a female now, when she ascends she will take on the properties of a male and ascend into her own. When you think of the souls being created, as you have been told, they were androgynous. Then they split as you have read or been told. One of the souls would be male and the other female and they would go out on their separate journeys to gain more consciousness and enlightenment. When that was completed, they would come back and join once more.

During the time when the androgynous pair split, one would be the male and one the female, but both would carry the two principals within them. And as I was saying, this Channel's soul is male and when she meets up with her other half, her flame, that would be the female part of her. This is a difficult concept for people, for their mind gets into it trying to find a mental picture to match all of this.

Some of you may think you will just change over night while in your bed. If you are a female you could wake up with a beard and a penis. Well, that really would be weird, would it not? However, when you ascend you will have more of your original soul's energy and you will change form.

How can I make this where it is clearer for people? You have read when a person dies, we will say around the age of 60, and this is not this Channel's age in case you are wondering, when a person dies on his/her journey to Nirvana, the person immediately starts dropping the dross energies of the Etheric body. He or she becomes the age of around 30-35 which is usually the height of health for most people.

Therefore, when you ascend, a similar situation can happen. You drop the female aspects and gather in the male aspects. Now this can happen on board the space-ship in the Rejuvenation Chambers where you will have your body healed and come out in all your glory of your original soul. This Channel, therefore, will come out in her male form in her male robes and meet her flame who is a female.

It is so difficult to describe something to someone who does not have a previous experience of it. An obvious example could be a flower. You have never seen a particular flower, but when you see it for real, you can appreciate it. When this Channel went to Hawaii years ago, she saw for the first time those beautiful Antherium flowers with the long stamen. Their nickname is the *boy flower*. They are usually red or pink and have a glossy leaf-shaped flower with a long yellow stamen. That was her first experience with this type of flower.

Therefore, until you have seen and experienced it, you do not know it. This is what is happening with this change in gender for humanity. Comically, you can look at your relatives or friends and imagine how they will look as a male or female. And start hoping if you are going to change to a male that you will have your hair and that you will not have too much of a beard, for women have spent hours in a salon getting waxed from the straggly whiskers that stubbornly have appeared.

Therefore, there is some humor for you at the same time. However, it is all about balance; it is all about getting you ready for your ascension. We have said that ascension is similar to stepping through another door. Some people will not realize that they have ascended. There is a veil of forgetfulness also so that people could forget that they were once a female 24 hours ago and now they are a male.

Until you have actually have gone through it, it is difficult to explain to you, and I hope you have a little more clarity on this now. It is an amazing time in history—an amazing time. Those of you who are Fundamentalist Christians may not understand this or else you will equate it with the rapture—being taken up to Heaven. That is not totally correct. There is a difference here. People will equate it to the Rapture for they will be in bliss when they rise up.

This book is not about the Rapture (*a questionable occurrence*), but of the principals—the feminine and masculine principals and how they must be balanced. And if you are a female, you will become a male and if you are a male, you will become a female, going back to your soul essence. You have taken on many lifetimes where you were one gender or another, learning your lessons, honing in on how it was to be a male or how it was to be female. This is one of your greatest lessons that you have learned. Now that you have learned it, you will be dropping down into your original state becoming the original gender of that soul. Those of you who are walk-ins and have chosen a different gender, your karmic agreement was to help that body/soul to return to its original state.

Therefore, dear ones, the entire planet will be under- going a physical change. Each person has agreed to do this. Those people who have already passed on in their particular female or male body were not ready yet to join their original state. Therefore, they went on ahead and they can come back at another time or they can go on to other planets—whatever they wish.

Therefore, dearest Readers, that is why it has been so important for you to make your choices, to make those decisions to come off of that fence and why you have been told it is almost too late to do so for there is so much involved—so much.

I am going to name this chapter, *The Gender Equation by Yeshua.*

All right dear one that is it for today. I AM Yeshua.

(Author: I urge you to read the Appendix where Yeshua's lecture is presented with Cynthia's kind permission.)

10 - MARY MAGDALENE'S INSIGHT

Good morning, my precious ones, ***I AM Yeshua,*** *come once again to continue on this book. It is almost finished. We noticed this morning—this bright sunny morning in Arizona—that people are being affected by the energies throughout the planet. Some have just unusual lethargy; they feel like they want to sleep all of the time and/or are not functioning on all four burners. We say to you it's the energies on the planet, dear ones. Try not to worry about it, and follow your body's instructions. If it wants to rest, then rest. If it wants you to eat something that you have not eaten for a long time and wonder why you have a craving for it now, eat it. It is your body telling you what you need to know and to do in order to ride this wave of ascension. I will now step back. We have another Being to come forth, do we not? I spoke last in Chapter 9, so we will now have a woman with the feminine energies in order to have balance in this book.*

Dear ones, it is I, **Mary Magdalene,** back once again. We do pop in and out, do we not? This chapter is for the purposes of bringing you more or less up to date on your process. You have read or heard on the Internet, and almost all of those contributors are speaking about the coming ascension, you have heard it will be in 2012. Some people are saying it is 2011—11-11-11 (November 11, 2011). There may be some truth to that, dear ones, but we still say that the majority of you will be ascending on December 21, 2012, and beyond.

Energy is never cut and dried. Think of a river rushing along, rapidly flowing over your pathway. You wish to cross over to the other side of the river—ascension. Now, where do you cross? If you cross some place up stream, you could label that 2011. If you crossed further down, you could label that 2012. And if you chose to cross even further down the river, you could label that crossing 2017. Do you understand?

You could be going to your ascension in different increments. It does not necessarily have to be in a flood of energy, for each person does it at his/her own time, even Mother Earth. She will take her time and her timing will be correct. So when you read/hear that this will happen in 2011 or this will happen in 2013, just know that that is as close as **they** think it will be. Energy is constantly flowing. It makes it very difficult to pin-point an exact time. However, at this point we are saying **December 21, 2012**.

Some of you have wondered how the UFO situation plays into all of this. You all know and have heard of the Ashtar Command with Commander Ashtar (*and Admiral Sananda*), I am sure. And YES, his ships are still circling the planet, almost into the millions at times. He/they watch over the different situations that are playing out around the planet.

When a particular head of a country is getting agitated and has his finger posed over a nuclear device of some kind, the Ashtar Command can instantly negate that action so that whatever button is pushed will instantly malfunction. You are being watched over, dear ones; you are being watched over. The planet is guarded in that sense. This is with the full permission of the Supreme Being. No one wants this Earth to be decimated with nuclear devices—no one.

This Channel happened to briefly watch Trinity Broadcasting Network (TBN). They were talking about the many prophecies and Armageddon. The pastors were so sure all the prophecies that the horsemen were symbolizing would take place, including the Rapture. We say hear that with a grain of salt. The pastors follow all of that in the Bible, but it is not going to be as explicit as they are preaching. There will be trials and tribulations and some attempts at war, but there will not be the devastating World War III that is predicted in the Bible.

You see, the Fundamentalists do not realize that when they put such an emphasis on the negative aspects that are prophesized—Armageddon—they put fear into people's hearts. Now they think that is a good thing, but we say that fear goes out, touches that Ring-Pass-Not and bounces back having multiplied with everyone else's fear. Now, has that been a service for the planet? Has that been a blessing in anyway—that fear has been multiplied throughout the countries? NO, NO.

We suggest to not fantasize these different scenarios. Try not to picture the ways that these prophecies could play out. It is best to not even think of them. People are so afraid that Iran is going to do this and Israel will retaliate; people just blow it out of proportion. Do not put any energy into all of this, dear ones. Let it play out and know you are protected. The Ashtar Command has a direct edict from the Supreme Being. Have faith in your soul that you will be in the right place at the right time and then go on with your life, living the good life to the best of your ability.

Now, let us address something else. Let us address the fact that some say people need to store up food; or they need to store up water. For a while this Channel kept a large box of different foods in a closet. She had some half gallons of water stored away. That was a couple of years ago. However, now she has decided *I do not have to worry about that anymore. I do not believe there will be lack. There is no lack in the Father's House. Therefore, my soul will provide for me.* She actually believes this. Consequently, you see, what she is doing is practicing the *Law of Attraction*. She knows **for her** there will be no lack. She has simple tastes, although when people walk into her house they think she comes from wealth. But much of what they see in her house is what she has brought with her from the home of her parents who loved the old Victorian style—(*14 rooms filled with antiques*).

However, this Author has very simple tastes. She is satisfied with a Power Bar for breakfast. At other times she may go to a restaurant and have a large meal around mid-afternoon. Then at dinner time, she maybe has a half a bread-stick stuck in some peanut butter. Therefore, with tastes that simple, she does not have to worry about food. She has the Reverse Osmosis for her water supply. She does not worry, for she knows she will be led and taken care of. That is the attitude for people in this day and age.

Do not go to a store and buy everything off the shelf and hoard the food so that **you** will have it. It is not necessary and we say that when you hoard that way, you bring to you the very thing you are trying to escape. You are bringing to you lack, for you would no sooner eat all of that or drink all of that up than you would have to go back to the store. Now the shelves are bare, for someone else has hoarded and has bought it all up and cleaned the shelves off. Do you understand, dear souls? Do not perpetuate lack when there is none.

There can be periods where a particular item has not made it to the stores. But now you get to use your flexibility. If your particular brand is not available, then try another brand. There will always be supplies and food on the shelves in your stores. Believe that; believe that.

Now I am going to address something else. It is time, dear souls, where it is imperative to give yourself what the Lord Sananda calls *still time*. It is the time when you still yourself; you sit and contemplate. You can be on a foam raft in your swimming pool. Just give yourself an hour of peace with no interruptions and just still yourself. You will be surprised at what thoughts will come to you. Those thoughts could very well be a Master making contact with you. There are hundreds of prospective channels just waiting to have what we will call their *radio waves* recognized. If you are not opened to hearing the Masters, why would they come to you? If you are forever racing around to movies, shopping, or whatever, why would they come to you? They come to you when you provide a time slot for them, when you are quiet, or maybe when you are listening to some uplifting music—something to keep you quiet.

Now since this Channel channels what she hears and turns that into books, she provides that space for us to come. She has soft music playing; she sits on her little love seat in the bay window of her bedroom. The energies are all set. She has said a prayer to the Father. She has brought in the prayer of Forgiveness. She has brought in the Violet Flame. She pictures herself standing in the energy flow of the Father. She opens her channels and calls forth for the higher Beings to come. And that is when we come; that is when Yeshua comes and makes his salutation. Therefore, you see, everyone needs time to be still so that we may come and speak with you.

You see, some people do not realize this, but they are actually providing a service for us and humanity. How can we get our messages across if no one will open to us and allow us to speak with them? If they are advanced enough to allow us to speak with them, would they not then share what they have just heard? They would not just sit and talk with us and then go on their way and never tell anyone about our messages. NO, they write it down or tape it and then transcribe it on the computer so it can be printed out. It then can become a book or they could pass the pages to people to read. You see how the messages could go out. So many people are being led to write books these days and why do you think that is? It is because their soul is opening the centers of the body, saying it is time now for me to be of service to these higher Masters. It is time; it is time, humanity—hundreds and thousands of you have this ability and yet you do not know it. Or if you have this ability, you have such doubts that it could possibly happen to **you** that you **keep** it from happening. You think it is just you ruminating in your head. Sometimes it is. But so often it is the higher energies making a connection. Now granted, there could be dark energies wanting to make contact, but that then becomes a learning lesson for you. You will all go through that type of testing as this Channel has done. Nobody just sits down and starts channeling the Masters for a book without having prepared him- or herself for years. Even though you may not have realized it, you have been preparing yourself for years and eons of time from other past lives. You would have been channels then—great channels of noted worth.

This book is about the balancing of energies, the importance that it is right now and being of service. Opening yourself up brings into play the different energies—principals. It makes you conscious of them, and it brings that knowingness to you so that, if you have not already done so, you will start practicing being aware of the different energies that flow **in** your body and keeping them in balance. Keep them in balance, Readers, for that is all part of your ascension.

You know, when you go to drive your car, does it not need to have not only you at the wheel, but does it not need to have its spark plugs clean, its oil flowing, its tires full of air, the engine humming? All of these things need to act in unison and to be kept functioning. That is why so often a vehicle is a metaphor for your own body. As you keep your car clean in every aspect, so do you keep your body. In fact if your car is grungy and you throw fast food cartons in the back seat and your ash tray is full of cigarette butts or you have tissue thrown all over the floor, nothing has been dusted and you barely can see through the windshield, is that not a metaphor for what your body looks like in and out? Yes, you may shower, but what is inside of your body? Think about that.

When this Channel was in graduate school years ago, she had a professor who taught the class that one could always tell what a person is like by how the inside of his or her car looks; or, the professor went on, how that person keeps his or her bedroom. These are all symbols of your body. Your house can be a metaphor for your body also. Are the rooms cluttered or do you have your stuff contained? Have you cleaned or is there dust over everything—all metaphors for your body's condition.

Of course, you can have some books lying here or there. Everything does not need always to be picked up. But on the whole, one does not need to have to take a shovel in order to make a path throughout your house either. (*You may see this example in a teenager's room.*) These are all metaphors for your body. Where is the balance? There is none. Keep this in mind so that when you drive your car, you can ask yourself if your car shows a positive example of your body. *Does my **house** look like a beautiful balance of my body?* Both of these are metaphors and very useful.

All right, dear Readers, we have just short little chapters in this book. We have done that on purpose, for sometimes when someone sits and reads a book such as ours, they skim it front and back; they might read it hither and yon. However, if the chapters are too long, they do not finish them. Therefore, by having short chapters, we hope people will continue reading. *It is only 7 pages; I have time for that.* And they will read what is meant to be given to them in that particular chapter.

Thus, you see, there is a method to our madness (*chuckles*)—short chapters, very simply stated but with powerful thoughts.

With that, dear Readers, I have finished my piece for today and I thank you for your time in reading this chapter.

I AM Mary Magdalene.

(*Oh thank you, Mary, that was fun.*)

You are welcome, dear one. And then there are Virgos who are too picky, are there not? (*Chuckles)*

(*Yes, laughing. That is something I am learning—to be not quite so meticulous.*)

It is always fun to bring in some humor with it also. All right, dear one, I bless you. Au revoir.

That was the love of my life and she brought in several observations that needed addressing for our book. So that is it for today, dear one. You have this to type up and you are working on the Appendix, so you have quite a bit of work to do. I bless you, dearest one.

I AM Yeshua.

CONCLUSION

Hello, my precious Readers, and to this Channel**. I AM Yeshua.** This morning we are going to bring this book to a close, for we see that we have inundated you enough with the teachings and thoughts on how you must balance the masculine and feminine energies within yourself. This must be balanced, dear ones, and we hope that we have given you that information so that you can take it into your body, into your mind, into your heart—so that you understand the importance of this.

We have brought you through 10 chapters. We have brought and alternated the feminine energies and the masculine energies with our Presenters—probably more so than in any of the other books. We were practicing what we were teaching; we were walking the talk with you. There was always a balance, so if we had the feminine energy for one chapter, we brought forth the masculine energy for the next chapter. Do you see how that works, dear ones?

You have come an extraordinary way in your progression in evolution. You are ready for your ascension. I will make this statement: I truly believe that all of you Readers who read these books are ready for ascension. Each one of you is being guided; each one of you is being given dreams, just as this Channel was given at the beginning of this book. These dreams guide you; they light up for you what needs to be done.

My Mary Magdalene was telling you in the last chapter how you can use different things in your life as metaphors for your body. That is so true.

Check your cars, everyone; check your bedrooms; check your houses—the metaphors for a body. See if all is clean and pure. Can anyone come into your house and be delighted with the feelings of the energy? People who come into this Channel's house remark, *oh, Jesus lives in this house.* It is not said in a religious tone. She has beautiful paintings of me, a large painting hanging in the living room and another one in her bedroom. She has a small one propped at the corner of her TV set. Every time she watches TV she glances at me and feels my energy.

These are all helpful in sustaining high energy in your house. Not everyone has to have pictures of me around their house, but just know when you have made a deep connection with me, my energy remains in those pictures. You will feel me and I am always with you—always.

These paintings I am referring to are from Glenda Green in Sedona, Arizona. I appeared to her and asked her to paint me—twice I did this. Therefore, you will have the young version of me holding a lamb and another version as an older, man looking at you—older and wiser, shall we say. I had to go through the third dimension physicality just as all of you have had to do.

How does one end a book such as this? How does one conclude these energies, these teachings from the Masters Most High? I will say I will conclude it as simply as I can. A conclusion is an end of some kind. Therefore, I am ending this book, but I end it on a note of joy, of thanksgiving, of appreciation. You have given me so much by just reading to the end. You have given me so much by just listening.

Many times when you pick up my books, I can remember the times when we were meeting back in that Biblical era. You sat at my feet, not because I was more than you, but you sat at my feet because we had no chairs. We were outside. And I perched myself on a rock. Sometimes I went up a hill so that people could see me better and that my voice would carry. However, it was not because I was above all of you. That was not my reason; it was merely so that you could hear me. Many times, as people know, in Israel the wind can blow. It blows right off the sea so that it is quite windy at times and will lift your voice away from your mouth so that others may not be able to hear you. That was my reason, dear souls.

The Goddess energy is on the planet now. It used to be patriarchal, you know. Look back at your history and you can see that with all the infamous warriors, such as Genghis Khan—infamous warrior and not always acting for the betterment of mankind—and Alexander the Great, a warrior and a conqueror. They had little Goddess energy. They had what we would call *street smarts,* for they were very clever. They knew how to wage war; they knew how to entrap people. That is the negative aspect. They used their masculine energy principal to its utmost. They loved it. They used that energy in an abrasive way.

Now civilizations are making a comeback as that Goddess energy permeates everything. It is love; it is intuition; it is creativity. The Goddess energy is one not to be ignored, dear friends, for if you ignore it, you have taken away your intuitive ability. You have taken away your creativity; you have taken away the caring and the gentle aspects of yourself. Keep that in mind. Your masculine energy, the strong one, helps you move through life. You must not have one over the other. All must be balanced before you can ascend.

That is all I wish to say, dear ones. As this Channel has told you, I will be coming back to write what we can call *My Memoirs (Chuckles).* I will be coming through the voice-channel, Cynthia Williams, and this Channel, Chako, will be my Scribe, for I can trust that she will guarantee that my words will be made into a book. We trust her that she will carry forth and get the book published. Each Channel is important to the task that the three of us will bring forth.

It is not necessary in this Conclusion to have others speak. It would be more or less overkill because you Readers can digest just so much of a new concept at a time. You will come to understand what I have meant in these teachings. As you go forward in your ascension, you will understand, dear ones, for it is evolution of the soul. All eventually will be on the same page.

With that, dearest Readers, thank you with all of my heart for allowing me to come and spend this time with you. You are precious to me and I hold you in my heart forever.

I AM Yeshua.

All right, dear one, we've done it!

(Yes, we have, laughing. We've done it, indeed! Thank you, Yeshua, for bringing all of the beautiful souls with you. They all had wonderful things to say, and I appreciate the honor of doing this for you and the Readers.)

You are welcome, dear one, and we will meet again in our 10th book. Bless you, dear one.

I AM Yeshua.

EPILOGUE

I started channeling this book on March 10, 2010. I finished Yeshua's dictation on Sunday, May 2, 2010. I usually feel sadness when I have completed a book, but this time, I just feel joy. It is because now we have a clear playing field for when Yeshua starts his dictation to Cynthia Williams, voice-channel, and to me, scribe, what we're calling for now *My Memoirs*, come mid-June. How exciting to listen and interact with this great Lord once again as he tells his story (his-tory) way before the Jesus era. But one book at a time—this one.

The front cover is a picture of me when I was 5 years old. I thought she expressed perfectly the innocence and shyness of the Goddess as she returned to Earth and stirred to life within all man/womankind. As you can see, she is not threatening in any way. She is merely waiting for recognition.

This book flowed nicely from chapter to chapter. I sat about 2-3 times per week. I would do the transcribing on a page or even a half of page at a time, accommodating my back as it painfully healed from a fractured vertebra (2-14-10). I have a mantra: *this too shall pass!* That is why I have such a sense of satisfaction. I was able to persevere and finish the project.

This book is also a short book, but oh, the puzzlement it will garner—hence the Appendix. I have no doubt you will need to study that and reread it several times.

As Yeshua said, *we've done it!* Yes, we have and I hope you enjoy it as much as I have enjoyed bringing this information to you. Until we meet again in Book 10…

I AM Chako (5-03-10).

NOTES

APPENDIX

***On 4-18-10, Jeshua ben Joseph** held his monthly class at my (Chako's) house. He comes through the voice-channel, **Cynthia Williams**. It is with her kind permission that I am able to bring this information to you Readers. The following is the **Question and Answer** period. My question on the masculine and feminine principals generated much discussion as we students grappled with this new information.*

Chako: I heard one of your lectures when you were talking about the masculine and feminine principals that we need to bring into balance and that **if we are a female, we must ascend as a male, and if we're a male, we must ascend as a female**. I don't understand that statement.

Jeshua: Thank you, my beloved sister, and I will clarify that. In your **first** journey upon the earth, if you came in as a male, you did the step-down process in male form. Then in order to bring balance to yourself, because your blueprint was male coming in,—your journey down here, not a right or wrong, please understand that—and you're about ready to come back out, you're going to come back out in your female form, so this brings the two into balance within you. Do you understand?

Now, if you're in a relationship and you're with a male and the male came in as a female, you came in as a male, you're joined together, and due to the work, you're going to ascend together, but you'll be in the form you need to be to balance that within one another, within self. Do you see?

Everything is about coming into balance in order to ascend. So if you came in one way, as a male, it is important that you ascend the other way, because truly in these higher realms, it becomes androgynous.

Do you understand? (To a point, I'm not quite sure whether you're speaking physically or ...) I'm speaking both, my beloved. So let's use Cynthia's body. Her body came in with a male soul. She is doing the ascension now as a female body. Once the ascension occurs and she is fully enlightened and has her God-Self fully anchored in, she's in balance with her male and female parts. At that point in time, she can choose to stay on the **new** earth plane as a female/male or further ascend. It is a choice (*from then on*).

What about beloved Quan Yin? Quan Yin ascended as a male and then came back as a female. Do you understand? But Quan Yin came in as a female, eons ago, ascended as a male but chose to embody and hold that of compassion as a female, because she felt at that point, she was totally in balance with herself; she would reach more of humanity in her Goddess self. Do you understand? Does that add the clarity? And what are you still questioning?

(Chako: I'm trying to put myself into that scenario, figuring it out.) All right, my beloved. You are working on your ascension, are you not? (Yes) You came in as a male soul in a female body. You're going to go out as a female. In the process of going out, you're bringing back the male part of you to bring it into balance. (So how does that line up with our being told we would be meeting our flame, who is perhaps another aspect?)

Jeshua: All right, my dear, when I was speaking of bringing that male energy in, before you can join with your flame, there has to be a balancing within you. So you can still meet up with your flame, but to bring the flame into you before you balance your male and female parts that you've done in the journey here upon the earth, that would keep you incomplete. So you've surmised in your mind that in my female form I'll bring my flame back and then I'm a whole. But that's not how it is. **You must balance both parts of yourself.**

The other night this Channel woke up at two in the morning. *As she woke up a male presence was entering her body.* Immediately she put out the call, frightened, because she could feel herself shifting. What she was told by Dr. Peebles, her guide, then was *Oh, dear, do not worry. That is your male side coming into balance with you because you are ascending.* It does not mean she will not be in balance. But *what do I need more of in my life to bring my masculine into balance with the feminine?* What do you think you need to do here?

But you see, my dear ones here in the room, this is a great way to ask *am I in balance; am I in joy in myself?* Or *have I allowed everyone's state of existence to influence me?* Back in Lumeria, my beloveds, when you were in fifth and sixth densities, please understand your way of procreating was not like it is now. Your vaginal areas and the man's penis areas were not developed in the same way. They only became a part of the step down process to experience the root chakra to help you remember what bliss was. Back in these particular time periods that I speak of, you procreated very much with touch.

This light within the beloved sister here, placing her hands upon somebody who was in pain and the pain was gone.... You will find a blissful state of existence. But for some of you, see, you haven't really had the opportunity to live out a blissful state with the opposite sex. So your next level will be to figure out what that's like. You see? If you take that from you and then say you have to go into androgyny it would rob you of the Ascension ladder, and the bliss in being able to be with a counterpart and experience that. Do you understand my beloved? Yes, I understand there is a lot here.

Q: Okay, what I don't understand clearly... Are you taking this existing body or how does it work (?)?

Jeshua: It depends, my beloved, do you want to take this existing body into the ascension? I'm going with... The true self is on board within that body. You can do that. At that point you will cease to age. Your body will "youth" itself. It will reverse age. And you will still stay in the body because you've ascended in it. It's a choice you have. Or you may lay down your body, still ascend, and come back with a new one. It's up to you.

For Cynthia here, I will use her again as an example. At age 60, she will cease to age. It will stop. She will not die. She will live on. But she will no longer age because she will not be a part of that belief structure any longer. At that point in time, she has asked that her body's blueprint be restored to that of a 30 year old individual. Healthy. And that she stays in female form. Now that's her request. You will all have that choice, but it is a gift that is given to you now that you are ascending.

Q: Without all this knowledge, at one point I started asking for 36 years old. I didn't know what I was doing, but it's just...

Jeshua: Because it's a gift for this ascension. See, you were becoming your God-Creator. You can have what you desire. But it must be felt within the heart. Many of you want to stay on to be of service. Many of you want to play upon the earth plane. All of you have played, but in a different realm of existence, while many of you want to stay and help those who haven't gotten here yet. So you will be prepared to do that. The world is more beautiful in what's coming than you can possibly comprehend. What you heard in the scriptures about the Garden of Eden will be returned upon the earth but improved upon.

There will be a balance within the systems upon the planet. You won't have barren deserts; they will once again bloom. Everything will become lush and fertile. Temperatures will be in balance—because you're in balance, you see, my beloveds. You have brought yourself to the state of balance. The imbalance began in the step-down process. But you chose to do that to help those who have lost their way.

You have much to look forward to. You have many tools that you can use. And even though you are sitting in your own houses, you can bring healing to the entire world with the tools that you have been given. If you see somebody who's murdered somebody on the news, drop into your heart, call forth the *Law of Forgiveness*, and call forth the balance to be restored there. You can do that for another. You're not controlling; you are activating a law that I brought forth. Do you understand?

Q: What is the time frame here for this?

Jeshua: 2012. 2012 begins the new cycle. But you understand the new cycle doesn't mean you're full blown. By **2017** you've got a good handle on what that new cycle is about. The new cycle requires you live from the heart. In order to really flourish the way you want to, it is to make your choices based upon the heart, not upon the mind. The mind is to serve the heart, but your heart knows what is right. You see? (*Yes*) You can feel it. When you ask that, the greater mind is Source, where all things are known simultaneously.

Celebrate your lives, my beloveds, for you are ascending. And you are part of the new creation, the new world. The new world is based on great integrity. This is why you're going through certain trials now. Do you stay in integrity? It's a test. The one you must answer to is you. You do not answer to Father, my beloveds. You answer to your own I AM Presence. That is the one that determines whether you're heading to rejoin your true power. Not because you've done anything incorrect, but because that **would destroy the universe if you took all your power before you had balanced yourself**. You would not have balanced with your male and female. If the male was in an aggressive state, it can cause harm, not only to you, but to others around you. It is not power over, it is power with. It is no longer win-win; it is co-creation. Win-win still means somebody had to win in order to feel good about the other person winning.

What is co-creation? Co-creation is *if you're happy, I'm happy* because it's the circle of life. You see? It is value within you. You value you, you value the other. You must come into balance within yourself. **To ascend, this is the law—to be in balance.** And if you are out of balance, you'll feel it right away, and you'll go back into balance. (Take in a deep breath.)

How many of you get up in the morning and thank yourselves because you are here? How many of you touch your body lovingly? It is a vehicle with an intelligence that has served you over and over again. Thank your body; love it. You will find your body responds to your gratitude. It will work better. The elementals within you, that make your body up, your vehicle, are very pleased to be loved. Disease, death comes about because of discord—discord of thoughts. Anything that isn't a match in you as the creator and the created and great love is discord. Do you understand?

What is there not to be happy about? We're here. You're helping to bring about a blueprint for others in other galaxies. You've done your job well and are continuing to do it. You may have loved ones who have their difficulties, and you may have certain physical difficulties, but I guarantee you, the more you use transmuting the violet flame, the more into harmony you become, and the less discord there is and the disease goes away. And you can do it for your loved ones.

Now, I want to say this: **75 percent of karma and discord is in the consciousness (*of humanity*).** It's a belief structure: **25 percent is personal**. So every time you call forth for humanity to have the violet flame instituted, and you begin to work within the consciousness of all that exists, you are helping to clear the discord. There is very little that's been left for a person to do except to deal with their own, and that makes the pressure upon them much easier because they're not weighted down. If they don't know the law, they're not able to deal with it and make their next ascension. Those of you who know the law can go to work with it and can clear what's in the atmosphere. That brings about Nirvana. That brings about the Great Garden. The blissful state of 2012 cannot happen until the discord is taken care of.

Does Mother Earth need to have her disasters? There's a certain part that will occur. Does it need to be to the extent that's been talked about? NO. It's already been postponed since last month (*March, 2010*) when I last was here. And in this way the Light is spreading out as more and more souls reclaim it. More and more individuals are calling forth for help. And every time a person makes that call, it alters the outcome. Do you understand my beloveds? Because you **are** the creators, you see? That is what I came to show you.

So you call it forth from Mother Earth, the violet flame, for her—compassion for her. That helps her. You call it forth for your children. **You work on you**. You affect lifetimes upon lifetime.

Jeshua: There are many rooms within the house *(body)* of each of you. Some of the doors have been closed to those rooms. It requires you to start opening the doors. Inch by inch you will do that. Your higher self is working with you to open the door when you're ready. Do not judge the experience of not being able to feel. Just know there are still some doors within you and they're still shut. When you're ready, you will open them.

Q: Is it necessary then for us to retrieve and follow the other aspects of ourselves and set intention for that to bring us into full alignment?

Jeshua: That's a wonderful question, my beloved. right now, for you who sit here, you are a composite of all the other aspects of you. All you must do is put forth a call that anything that is still out there that would serve in the ascension process that needs to come on board, come on board. And everything else be released back to the Great Creator. And then you work with what's right here, right now. That's it. (*Thank you.*) Pretty easy, isn't it? (*Yes*) Your path, your past life-times are all collapsing because it was built upon discord. As you dissolve the discord, by the tools that have been given, nothing can exist that's kept alive because of the discord. Do you understand? (*Yes.*) When you no longer dance in that arena, you no longer choose the drama because you remember who it is you are. There's nothing to keep it alive. It's like taking the air out of a balloon.

Jeshua: I joined with my Christed-self, which is the gateway to my I AM Presence. When I ascended, I ascended fully into my I AM Presence and at that point I ascended into Father, which is connected to the same. It is confusing for humanity to understand this process. So I will try to demonstrate with my hands here.

My earth self was here. The Christ-Self was here. I merged with the Christ-Self when I began my mission to create the energy around the planet of the Christ Consciousness, which is a Principal. It must be adhered to in order to connect back with your God-Self. For once I merged in my work with my Christ-Self, then the crucifixion took place and I then joined with my God-Self, which is above the Christ Self as I became One. Putting it on like a suit of clothing, coming into me, to stand fully in my power. Father, the energy of all things, was present and we are One. That energy is all of you. Let me give it to you another way. If none of you existed, it's not possible, but if none of you existed, would Father exist? Father wouldn't exist. Do you understand that, my beloved sister? If the cells of your body did not exist, would your body exist? But it is the cells coming together, in their I AM Presence, that creates the form. The form then has an experience. Do you understand? So who's created that sense of humor? Energy can never be destroyed; it can only change form. When I ascended, I ascended back into my I AM Presence, into All That Is. I never felt it was the earth-self doing the work. That's why I said, it's the Father that works through me; it is not I. It is the energy of All That Is that runs through me that does the work, for I am but a human. If I am not connected, I myself could do nothing. But the flow of energy through me could do everything. For I am then not in individualized form, I AM Oneness Form. And the Oneness Form is pure love.

All right, my beloveds. A beautiful Sunday afternoon, is it not? And every one of you here in the room, I've worked with this day. Your minds have expanded, and I've moved within your energy field and touched you, and remind you, we are together always. I am within you as you are within me. Go and have a beautiful afternoon. Dance. Laugh. Enjoy. My beloveds, you are loved and you **are** love. I thank you.

(*Sequence:* ***Earth-self_Christ-Self_God-Self_I AM Presence***.)

ABOUT THE AUTHOR

Verling CHAKO Priest, PhD was born in Juneau, Alaska, hence her name of Cheechako, shortened to just Chako by her mother, a medical doctor, and her father, an Orthodontist. Chako was raised in Napa, CA. She attended the University of California at Berkeley where she met her future husband. Upon their marriage and after his training as a Navy pilot, they settled into the military way of life. They lived twelve years outside of the United States Mainland in various places, which included Hawaii, Viet Nam, Australia, and Greece. Little did she know that these exotic lands and peoples were preparing her for her spiritual awakening years hence?

After her husband's retirement from the Navy, they resettled in Napa, California. It was during this time that she returned to school at Berkeley, transferred to Sonoma University where she earned her first two degrees in Psychology. Chako then entered the doctoral program at the Institute of Transpersonal Psychology (ITP) at Menlo Park, CA, which is now located in Palo Alto, CA. She successfully completed that program which consisted of a Master, as well as the Doctorate in Transpersonal Psychology. Ten years and four degrees later she was able to pursue her passion for Metaphysical and New Age Thought—her introduction into the realm of the Spiritual Hierarchy and the Ascended Lords and Masters.

In 1988, Dr. Priest moved to Minnetonka, Minnesota. She co-authored a program called, *Second Time Around* for those with recurring cancer for

Methodist Hospital. She, as a volunteer, also facilitated a grief group for *Pathways* of Minneapolis, and had a private practice.

She studied with a spiritual group in Minnetonka led by Donna Taylor (*now Fortune*) and the Teacher, a group of highly developed entities channeled by Donna. The group traveled extensively all over the world working with the energy grids of the planet and regaining parts of their energies that were still in sacred areas waiting to be reclaimed by them, the owners. They climbed in and out of the pyramids in Egypt, tromped through the Amazon forest in Venezuela, rode camels at Sinai, and climbed the Mountain. Hiked the paths at Qumran, trod the ancient roadways in Petra, Jordan, and walked where the Master Yeshua walked in Israel.

The time came, November 1999, when Chako was guided to move to Arizona—her next phase of growth. This is where she found her beloved Masters, who in reality had always been with her. They were **all** ready for her next phase, bringing into the physical several books—mind-provoking books, telepathically received by her, from these highly evolved, beautiful, loving Beings. Each book stretches her capabilities, as well as her belief systems. Nevertheless, it is a challenge she gladly embraces.

It is now May 2010. She just has finished writing her ninth book. She has been told that a tenth book will be started in June 2010. She will collaborate with Cynthia Williams. Yeshua will tell his life's story, his beginnings on Earth in the sea. Cynthia will voice-channel; Chako will scribe and bring all to fruition at Trafford Publishing.

Comments AZCHAKO@AOL.COM